The Life and Times of

James Nayler

The author is a Member of the Northumbria Area Meeting of the Religious Society of Friends (Quakers)

for my friend, Karenza Passmore

Hi Boss

Here's your copy
of the book I've
dedicated to you.

SW

North East Religious Le

A G

Thursda

10.00-12.30 Ebbe Room, C

01/17	**Register of Conflicts of Int**
02/17	**Minutes of the meeting he**
03/17	**Matters Arising from the 1**
11/16	Appointment o
12/16a	Executive Com
	Chair communi
	RRC pension c
13/16	Company Risk
14/16	Process
16/16	Partnership Agr
04/17	**Reports from the RRC Boar**

(a) Executive Committee
(1) Meetings with the St Hil...
St Hild and St Bede Trus
(2) Annual Staff Appraisals

Also from the Langley Press

James Nayler: The Quaker Jesus by George Whitehead
Elias Hicks: A Controversial Quaker
Deep Roots? A Fresh look at the Origins of Some Quaker Ideas
Quakers, Newgate and the Old Bailey
George Fox in Barbados
Susanna's Sisters: Early Quaker Women and the Sects of Seventeenth-Century England
The Life and Times of Jeremiah Dixon: Surveyor of the Mason-Dixon Line
The Quaker Sonnets
A Book of Quaker Poems
Our Name is Legion: A Quaker Memoir of Depression
The Theology of Small Things

For free downloads and more from the Langley Press, please visit our website at:

http://tinyurl.com/lpdirect

Contents

*For Jesus himself testified, that a prophet
hath no honour in his own country.*

(John 4, 44: all biblical quotations in this book are
from the King James Version, 1611)

The Life and Times of

James Nayler

The 'Quaker Jesus'

by

Simon Webb

From Ephraim Pagitt's *Heresiography*, 1661

Introduction

2016 turned out to be a good year to start writing a new book about James Nayler. That year was not only the three hundred and sixtieth anniversary of the event that defined history's view of the man: 2016 was also twenty years after Leo Damrosch published his *Sorrows of the Quaker Jesus* (which was not intended as a biography in any case), and thirty years since William S. Bittle brought out his Nayler book. Since then, both Quakerism, and historians' understanding of the early Quaker period, have changed.

Aids to understanding the enigmatic figure of the 'Quaker Jesus' now include new research into Nayler's military service, work on the importance of printing and publishing for the early Quakers, and twenty-first century views on the role of women in the first years of the society. Early Quaker women, including the controversial Martha Simmonds, had an important role to play in the extraordinary drama of Nayler's life.

2016 was also a good time to start writing about Nayler because the world he lived in was similar, in some surprising ways, to the world of the early twenty-first century. The seventeenth century in England was a time of rapid change, much of it extremely unwelcome to many of the English. Then as now, the function and legitimacy of well-established features of society were being seriously questioned, and undermined. To use a modern phrase, seventeenth-century policy-makers felt compelled to 'think the unthinkable' and re-shape the world to suit what they believed was happening beyond politics. Then as now, the economic basis of the lives of the English seemed shaky; as bad harvests, bad government and commercial challenges from abroad compromised the business of putting food in the mouths of the people. Then as now, political conflicts and international alliances meant that England became entangled in protracted, expensive and unpopular wars.

As in the early twenty-first century, the stresses of life were persuading some people that they should seek refuge in the perceived certainties of older ways of living and thinking. New religious groups like the Quakers claimed to be returning to the ways of the early Christians, and older groups such as the Anglicans, the Baptists and the Puritans were sometimes tempted to adopt a 'back-to-basics' approach, often with disastrous results. Many sects tried to use the Bible as a route-map for a way back to a simpler, better time, but the complexity and the self-contradictory nature of the Scriptures led to much confusion.

Like our own England, the England of the seventeenth century also had a problem with climate change. The world was then in the grip of a global cool period now called the Little Ice Age. For European economies, that were almost entirely dependent of agriculture, this had very severe implications, including the aforementioned disastrous harvests. Climate experts have determined that there was a particularly cold period in the middle of the century – the time of the end of the British civil wars, the execution of Charles I, the beginnings of Quakerism, and James Nayler's controversial ride into Bristol.

In his *Universal History*, the eighteenth-century French writer Voltaire included details of several cataclysmic political events that happened around this time, including the deposition of the Ottoman sultan Ibrahim, popular unrest in France, political problems with the Holy Roman Empire, and Spain's loss of Portugal and its empire.

Whereas today we would attribute crop failures and problems with the climate to scientific causes, English people in the seventeenth century were more likely to see such things as the judgement of God on a nation that had tried His patience. This was a habit of mind that Oliver Cromwell in particular seems to have embraced: he was a firm believer in divine providence. When the Scots made a tactical blunder at the civil war Battle of Dunbar in 1650, Cromwell is said to have declared, 'The Lord hath delivered them into our hands.' By contrast, political and military failures tended to confound the Lord Protector, albeit temporarily: was the Lord displeased with him?

Even people who did not attribute everything that happened to the will of God would still have been infected by the pervasive feeling of gloom, coldness, bleakness and hunger that was abroad at the time, because of the long, hard winters and disappointing summers.

Some seventeenth-century thinkers even extrapolated from the poor conditions they saw around them to speculate that there was a general and irreversible decline in every aspect of life. In his biography of the English poet John Milton, Samuel Johnson reminds us that:

There prevailed in his time an opinion that the world was in its decay, and that we have had the misfortune to be produced in the decrepitude of Nature. It was suspected that the whole creation languished, that neither trees nor animals had the height or bulk of their predecessors, and that every thing was daily sinking by gradual diminution.

Another feature of the seventeenth century in England that reminds us of life in the west today was the obscene gap between the incomes and life-chances of the rich and the poor. Since only a small proportion of the population (and no women at all) could cast their votes in parliamentary elections, there was also an extreme concentration of power, as well as money and property, in the hands of a few men.

It has recently become clear that in the democracies of the west, a number of politicians are quite prepared to use fear to motivate the people to think the way they want them to think. Fear of immigrants, particularly of Muslims, has been actively encouraged by some unscrupulous leaders, and this type of fear was also a major factor in the religion-bound politics of the seventeenth century in England.

Forced to become Protestants in the sixteenth century, many of the English had learned to fear Roman Catholics, and Roman Catholicism in general. Since several of the European powers who could pose a military threat to England were Catholic countries, the fear of people loyal to the pope coloured much of foreign policy in those days. Anti-Catholics tended to remember the St Bartholomew's Day

Massacre when their fear of Catholics was challenged. During that massacre, thousands of French Protestants, known as Huguenots, were killed.

As well as the widespread fear of Catholics, the British were also concerned that extreme sects which belonged somewhere on the Protestant side might also upset the *status quo*. While anti-Catholics remembered the French massacre of 1572, people who feared these newer sects would invoke events in the German town of Münster that had happened nearly thirty years earlier. There, an extreme Anabaptist sect took over the town and established what was supposed to be a kind of holy communism. Unfortunately, this meant that the town was subjected to a long siege. While the besiegers worked away outside, inside the walls the new ruler, John of Leiden, declared himself to be a new King David. John also legalised polygamy, and took sixteen wives.

The fears and obsessions of the public were often stirred up by the media of the time, much as politically biased tabloid newspapers in modern England can exacerbate political problems with alarmist headlines. The 'media' in seventeenth century England included speeches and sermons, some of which were controversial enough for the speakers and their followers to be arrested and locked up. There was also a bewildering number of books, pamphlets and news-sheets, many illustrated, some very poorly written. Many of these were designed to make a particular religious and/or political point, and some were written in direct response to slightly earlier papers with which the authors disagreed.

James Nayler was not above arming himself with a pen and fighting in the trenches of these 'pamphlet wars'. Though often crude in the extreme, these texts could be very influential. John Lilburne, of whom more later, managed to found and sustain the remarkable Leveller movement on the basis of the tracts which he regularly published; and these are thought to have been popular enough for Lilburne to make something of a living from the sales. This is not surprising, since it seems to have been relatively cheap to produce such pamphlets. George Fox, the founder of the Quakers, was evidently able to have a stock of such papers run up for himself, even when he had very little income. So thick was the torrent of controversial literature – which was perhaps the characteristic literature of the time – that the twentieth-century literary expert Herbert Grierson remarked that new poetry and plays had become a mere 'sparkling side-stream' throughout much of the seventeenth century.

The printing technology of the time had changed little since the German pioneer Johannes Gutenberg had first experimented with printing over two centuries earlier. The presses were large contraptions built mainly of wood, which often had to be braced to the ceiling of the room where they were located, because the forces involved in the printing process might otherwise cause the device to break apart.

Printing was driven by gravity and human strength, in those days before steam or electricity could be used to speed up the presses. Two men would operate the machine, one of them inking the forme (the equivalent of a modern printing plate) while the other worked the mechanism that allowed the paper to get in the right position to be pressed onto it. A printer's boy, called a 'fly', might perform additional tasks.

In theory, such a team of printers could produce two hundred or more printed sheets per hour, but the sheets processed at this rate would only be printed on one side: usually they would need to be 'backed up'; printed on both sides. The procedure was also slower than the figure of two hundred sheets an hour might suggest, because of course the forme had to be made up before-hand, and the paper had to be dampened to allow it to take up the ink. The printed pages then had to be dried, and assembled into a book or pamphlet; if they were not 'broadsides' - single sheets printed on one side.

Some of the surviving controversial literature from this period shows signs of having been printed cheaply, and put through the presses very hastily. Sometimes the printers seem to have spent little time 'making ready', which is the printers' phrase for the business of taking a series of test prints of a page and adjusting things to eliminate irregularities. As a result, many of these seventeenth-century tracts are very faintly printed in some parts, while other sections are extremely black and blobby, with the letters running into each other. In some cases, the sheets were poorly 'backed up' so that the reader can see the ink coming through from the other side.

Many of these texts would have been lost if it were not for George Thomason, a London bookseller and publisher who collected over twenty-two thousand of them between 1640 and 1661. The fragile originals of these so-called Thomason Tracts are now housed in the British Library's new building at St Pancras in London; but microfilm and online versions are widely available for researchers.

As well as offering a mirror to our own times, the story of James Nayler shares the special charm of Quaker history in general: at last, here is a type of history where the leading characters are not (for the most part) kings and queens or other types of aristocrats, and where the most significant actions in the characters' lives are not military campaigns. The best of early Quaker history is about quite ordinary people: tailors, printers, farmers, apprentices, shop-keepers and the like, whose extraordinary religious experiences caused them to step out from the darkness of obscurity into the light of history.

Where the early Quakers' own writings survive, for instance among the Thomason Tracts, or in letters, their way of writing, unmediated by hypocrisy or a sophisticated approach to composition, is often raw and direct, reflecting perhaps how they spoke rather than how formal English prose was 'supposed' to be written.

The 'coverage' of ordinary people's lives in early Quaker history is enhanced in comparison with the history of many other periods and movements because of the strong participation of women. For once, that half of the human population of the planet that is little heard in other areas of history is allowed to have a voice. As Kate Peters points out in her 2005 book *Print Culture and the Early Quakers*, these early Quaker women are much loved by historians because they are unusually visible to history. The reasons for this include the surviving writings of seventeenth-century Quaker women themselves.

The century of George Fox and James Nayler was a time when more writings by women, and not just Quaker women, were being published than had been the case before. According to Patricia Crawford, writing in Mary Prior's book *Women and English Society*, between 1616 (the year of Shakespeare's death) and 1620, only eight works by women (of any religious persuasion) were published, on average less than two a year. By contrast, between 1646 and 1650, sixty-nine works by female writers were published, or nearly fourteen per year.

During the 1650s, a crucial time in the life of both James Nayler and the early Quaker movement, nearly half of all women's published works were written by Quakers; but their contribution to Quaker literature at this time was small in comparison to that of Quaker men. In fact only six Quaker women wrote tracts in their own right: others contributed to collaborative works. Among the six were the aforementioned Martha Simmonds, who was central to Nayler's story; and Margaret Fell, the so-called Mother of Quakerism, who married George Fox in 1669.

Women writers and preachers were by no means found only among the Quakers: other sects had them too, notably the Brownists, the Baptists and the Fifth Monarchy Men. No doubt many of these women preachers were sometimes confronted with an old rhyme that stated:

When women preach and cobblers pray
The fiends in hell make holiday

This couplet is more apt to the early Quaker situation than may appear at first. As an apprentice to a shoe-maker, George Fox, the founder of Quakerism, could be counted as a cobbler. And strange to say, Jacob Boehme, a German mystic whose writings influenced early Quaker thinking, was also a shoe-maker. As we shall see, Boehme, who died in 1624, the same year George Fox was born, was published in English translation by Giles Calvert, one of the first publishers of Quaker books.

Women preachers had, however, to contend with more than just silly rhymes. In those days, the Bible itself was weaponised, and a passage from his first letter to the Corinthians, and another from his first letter to Timothy, were frequently used by critics of women's preaching to indicate that Saint Paul, at least, did not approve of women's ministry:

Let your women keep silence in the churches: for it is not permitted unto them to speak; but they are commanded to be under obedience as also saith the law.

(1 Cor 14, 34)

Let the woman learn in silence with all subjection. But I suffer not a woman to teach, nor to usurp authority over the man, but to be in silence.

(1 Timothy 2, 11, 12)

In her tract *Women's Speaking Justified*, published in 1666, Margaret Fell argued in favour of women's preaching, by putting the Corinthians passage into context, and taking advantage of the fact that the Bible is full of contradictions: despite Paul's opinion, there are many examples of women's ministry to be found in that book.

One of Margaret Fell's arguments in *Women's Speaking Justified* involves the women who discovered that Jesus' body was missing from its tomb after his crucifixion. These women were instructed to carry the news of the resurrection – the central event in the Christian narrative – to Jesus' followers.

In her tract, Margaret Fell put the Corinthians passage in context by identifying the occasion that led to the letter being written in the first place. Fell implies that this was a time of chaotic stress in the early church at Corinth: Paul might have thought that the women could calm things down a little by keeping quiet.

Fell claims that this is not a strategy that is appropriate to her own times, because, she asserts, a new age has now dawned. For many hundreds of years, from the ascension of Jesus into heaven to her own epoch, including the year when Paul's first letter to the Corinthians was written, the world has been ruled by the Beast and the Whore of Babylon, as described in the New Testament book of Revelation. But now the time of the Beast:

. . . is over, which was above twelve hundred years, and the darkness is past, and the night of apostasy draws to an end. And the true light now shines, the morning-light, the bright morning star . . .

In this new dawn, the 'spirit of the Lord Jesus' will be 'poured upon all flesh, both sons and daughters'.

Although James Nayler was sometimes close to Margaret Fell, and was indeed among the first Quakers she ever met, the published female Quaker writer who is of most interest to students of his life is Martha Simmonds; daughter of a country vicar, sister of a London printer, and wife of another London printer. Martha not only wrote: she also preached, and challenged other preachers, disrupting church services with her words. She also disturbed meetings led by Quaker preachers with whom she disagreed. As well as arguing in person and in print, Martha enacted 'signs' as a way of promoting her gospel message: she went through the streets of the ancient English city of Colchester in Essex, in sackcloth and ashes, and she tells us that she spent two years crying repentance in 'cities, towns, and market-streets'.

Martha Simmonds, of whom more later, was born at Meare, a village in Somerset, in 1624, the same year as George Fox.

As well as shedding a light on the lives of ordinary people, and of women in particular, for the benefit of historians, the early Quaker period is important to Quakers themselves because it was at this time that the society emerged and began to define itself. Because British Quakers have never had a formal creed or catechism, conversations about who the Quakers are and what they believe tend to bring in Quaker history. Like jazz music, it is hard to describe or define Quakerism, but anyone given this task might do well to use examples from Quaker history; much as someone asked to define jazz to an audience of listeners might resort to playing a few classic tracks to give his hearers a feel for the form.

The story of James Nayler is important as part of the definition of Quakerism not only because Nayler himself was a very important early Quaker but because, if things had gone differently, Quakerism might have developed in a different direction to the one it actually took, because of Nayler himself. As we shall see, early Quakerism spread with surprising rapidity, even when this speed was set against the unusually fast pace of events in seventeenth-century England. To use an analogy that may not be entirely appropriate to the 1650s; when a fast train comes off the rails, its various parts can end up further from the track than those of a slow train.

To give an idea of the pace of change in Nayler's England: a woman born in 1600 (i.e. a woman who belonged to George Fox's parents' generation) would have spent her first years during the reign of the glamorous English Protestant queen, Elizabeth I. At that time, there would still have been plenty of people around, including her grandparents, who would have remembered life under the Catholic queen, Mary, who had tried to reverse the English Protestant Reformation imposed by her father, Henry VIII.

When our child of the new seventeenth century reached the age of three, she would have been living under the rather less glamorous Scottish monarch, James I. By this time, England and Scotland had been united under one crown, though the cultural differences between the two countries would play out in alarming ways as the century progressed.

In her mid-twenties, our seventeenth-century woman would have found herself living as a subject of Charles I, a monarch who was quite over-matched by the challenges of his age. Charles did not have the intelligence or political insight of his father James I, or his son, Charles II. Despite (or perhaps because of) his inability to read the runes of his age, the first Charles tried to play political games that only a very intelligent, skilled and lucky monarch could have won.

In seventeenth-century England, as in the same country at the time of the medieval Wars of the Roses, uncertainty about the ultimate source of political power meant war. As our woman born in 1600 proceeded through her forties, Charles I and Parliament grappled in two disastrous civil wars, which had a profound effect on the British Isles in general, and on the life of James Nayler in particular.

As our 1600 lady neared fifty, the first Charles, defeated in war and tried for his crimes, stepped out of a window at the Banqueting House in London, onto a high scaffold that had been erected there. This happened in the early afternoon of the thirtieth of January 1649.

Given the vast changes that affected Britain in the seventeenth century, it is hardly surprising that Margaret Fell, in her *Women's Speaking Justified*, should have claimed that her own times were special and unique, and that there were signs that the apocalyptic events described in the book of Revelation might soon come to pass, complete with the destruction of the Beast and the Whore of Babylon, and the descent from heaven of the New Jerusalem.

The second edition of Margaret's *Women's Speaking Justified* was published in 1667, by which time London had been visited by a plague which killed perhaps a quarter of its population. Shortly after the plague petered out in 1666, the capital was hit by the Great Fire, which, though it is supposed to have killed very few people, still changed the face of the city forever.

Having died in 1660, James Nayler did not witness either the plague or the fire; but there were enough signs visible during his own life to suggest that something special was happening. In the words of Jesus himself:

. . . ye shall hear of wars and rumours of wars: see that ye be not troubled: for all these things must come to pass, but the end is not yet. For nation shall rise against nation, and kingdom against kingdom: and there shall be famines, and pestilences, and earthquakes, in divers places. All these are the beginning of sorrows. Then shall they deliver you up to be afflicted, and shall kill you: and ye shall be hated of all nations for my name's sake. And then shall many be offended, and shall betray one another, and shall hate one another. And many false prophets shall rise, and shall deceive many. And because iniquity shall abound, the love of many shall wax cold. But he that shall endure unto the end, the same shall be saved.

(Matthew 24: 6-12)

I. A Quaker Icon

It must be one of the most striking portraits ever produced in the form of an engraving. At first glance, it appears to be a picture of Jesus, as he is usually shown, as a young man with a beard and long hair. At the second glance, the viewer is, however, struck by the fact that this 'Jesus' is wearing a collar, doublet and cape in the style of men in seventeenth-century Europe. At the third glance, the viewer notices that this 'Jesus' has a capital 'B' on his forehead. A very close examination of the portrait reveals that there seems to be something odd about the set of the sitter's mouth. Is he dehydrated; does he have very bad (or missing) teeth, or could there be an injury to his tongue?

At this point, a Quaker with some knowledge of Quaker history might look over the viewer's shoulder and say, 'This is James Nayler, the Quaker who rode into Bristol, in October 1656, in such a way that it reminded people of Christ's ride into Jerusalem on Palm

Sunday. He was accused of blasphemy as a result of his ride, and his punishment was to be branded on the forehead, and to have his tongue bored through with a hot poker.' Both before and after this part of his multi-phase punishment, Nayler was also soundly whipped, so that between his neck and his waist the top layer of skin was almost completely removed.

The portrait has some of the intensity of the 1500 painted self-portrait of Durer, where the artist seems to be impersonating Jesus. Like the engraving of Nayler, Durer's picture shows a young man with a beard and long hair, and in both pictures the hair is straight until it reaches the level of the ears. It then becomes curly (in Durer's case) or wavy (in Nayler's). As we shall see, this is an important detail.

Both pictures seem to draw on the older tradition of portraits of Christ as the 'man of sorrows'. These pictures are inspired by a passage in the Old Testament book of Isaiah, and typically show Jesus looking downcast, with the crown of thorns on his head.

A version of this engraving of Nayler, by an anonymous artist, appears on page two hundred and forty-four of the 1661 edition of Ephraim Pagitt's book, *Heresiography*. The book is a catalogue of the many religious groups and ideas that the author considered heretical, and was something of a best-seller – the 1661 edition was the sixth, published the year after Nayler's death at the age of forty-four. In it, Pagitt presents Nayler as a representative 'Shaker or Quaker', and identifies the Quakers as 'an upstart branch of the Anabaptists, lately sprung up, but thickest in the North parts'. Pagitt goes on to say that 'this heresy is composed and made up out of the dregs of the common people'. Pagitt's description, as represented here, is wrong in almost every respect.

There are other portraits of Nayler, all of which, like the engraving in Pagitt's book, were probably executed by artists who never actually saw Nayler himself. An etching dated 1657, the year after Nayler suffered his brutal punishment, shows him looking much older and thinner, with a thicker beard and a low-set hat, perhaps to hide the branded 'B' on his forehead. The inscription under this portrait identifies him as 'the king of the Quakers', and he stands in front of a window through which we see him riding backwards on a horse: that is to say, riding facing the wrong way. This humiliating way of riding was forced on him during his return to Bristol after his punishment in London.

A similar portrait, but showing Nayler in rather better health, appears in a woodcut in a German book published in 1702. This shows Nayler standing with his contemporary Sabbatai

Sevi, a Turkish Jew who claimed to be the long-awaited Jewish Messiah. Since some felt that Nayler had deserved his punishment because he had claimed to be Christ, the Christian Messiah, it is not surprising that writers looking back on the lives of these two men should have seen similarities between them.

The 1657 engraving, and the one showing Nayler with Sevi, both feature royal regalia – crown, orb, sceptre and ceremonial sword – arranged on a table. This is a reminder of the royal connotations of both Jesus, and the Messiah of the Jews. For many Christians, Jesus is 'Christ the King', descended from the Old Testament King David, and not just a poor prophet and healer of the streets, roads, and fields.

A third, quite different, engraving of Nayler, supposedly based on a portrait by Rembrandt, appears as an illustration to a Dutch poem, *Klachte der Quakers*, published in 1657. Although the link to Rembrandt is probably fictitious, and the portrait bears no real resemblance to any other pictures of Nayler, the engraving in *Klachte der Quakers* is, nevertheless, a lovely piece of work. It shows a hirsute, rugged, middle-aged man, apparently exhausted, perhaps trying to come to terms with a piece of bad news, but retaining a kind of philosophical good-humour. The portrait could certainly be of a Yorkshire farmer, as Nayler was before he heard his Call, and given what we know about his life, it is likely that Nayler was often exhausted, and often in receipt of very bad news.

A German engraving from 1702 has none of the subtlety or ambiguity of the *Klachte der Quakers* picture. It shows the event that led to Nayler's punishment. Here Nayler, his head much too large for his body, looks more like Mr Punch than Jesus, or indeed any human being who ever lived. He is riding up to the gate of Bristol on an understandably shy-looking horse that is all out of proportion with itself, while hundreds of people, most of them women, look on, chanting 'Heilig'. Nayler's horse walks over flowers, branches and cloaks that have been placed before it, but the whole scene looks less like a seventeenth-century re-enactment of the events of Palm Sunday than a nightmarish puppet-play. Unfortunately, some later engravers seem to have based their idea of Nayler on his depiction here.

Continental interest in Nayler's case went beyond just Germany and the Netherlands, where the last two portraits mentioned above were produced. In book published in 2016, Brandon Marriott lists, and quotes from, accounts of Nayler not only from England, Germany and the Netherlands, but also Italy, France, Ireland and Turkey. Though he is little known today outside Quaker circles, James

Nayler was famous (some would say notorious) throughout Europe in the late seventeenth and early eighteenth centuries.

In publishing the anonymous engraving of Nayler with the 'B' visible on his forehead, Ephraim Pagitt was probably intending to show his readers what a pitiful condition sectarians could be reduced to if they persisted in following their doctrines. The short poem engraved under the picture in Pagitt's *Heresiography* implies that the author believed the theology of Nayler and his ilk was the worst kind of error a believer could fall into:

Of all the sects that Night and Errors own
And with false lights possess the world, there's none
More strongly blind, or who more madly place
The light of Nature for the light of Grace.

The meaning of the poem is not entirely clear, but if, as seems logical, we assume that Pagitt was forced by his metre to substitute the word 'place' for 'replace' in the third line, then the poem would appear to be saying that Nayler and his followers had mistaken something which we might call 'the spark of life' in themselves for the 'divine spark', the indwelling Christ, or the Quakers' 'that of God'.

Although the poem seems to be suggesting that we 'read' Nayler's portrait as something like a modern road-sign warning of a hazard, the skill that has gone into the engraving is sufficiently subtle for the viewer to see it in an entirely different light.

It is telling that the London National Portrait Gallery's version of this picture is on a page that was at some point cut out of a copy of Pagitt's book. Likewise, Leo Damrosch reproduces a page from a copy of *Heresiography* kept at the Harvard University library, from which the engraving and its poem have been cut out and replaced with a pasted-in hand-drawn sketch, and a copy of the poem in long-hand. Clearly, the people who mutilated these copies intended to do something with the engravings beyond merely looking at them whenever they happened to read that page of Pagitt's book. Could it be that at least one of these vandals removed the engraving so as to frame it and display it as a source of inspiration?

II. The Theatre of Cruelty

James Nayler's England, the England of the middle of the seventeenth century, showed many signs of civilisation, and indeed enlightenment. This was, after all, the world of the poets Milton, Marvell and Dryden, the philosopher Thomas Hobbes, John Bunyan (the author of *The Pilgrim's Progress*), the diarist John Evelyn, the biographer John Aubrey, the architect Inigo Jones, the scientist Isaac Newton, and the composer Henry Purcell. In many respects, however, the age was cruel and barbaric, as the punishment meted out to James Nayler demonstrates.

One of the best-known, and unfortunate, victims of the rough justice of the time was the Puritan writer William Prynne. In 1632 Prynne published his *Histriomastix*, subtitled *The Player's Scourge, or Actor's Tragedy*, a lengthy book detailing the many reasons why theatres and plays were bad ideas.

Unfortunately for Prynne, plays, particularly

the elaborate masques of the period, were an integral part of life at the court of King Charles I. Indeed Charles's wife, Queen Henrietta Maria, herself took part in a masque called *The Shepherd's Paradise* in 1633.

Prynne's *Histriomastix* was interpreted as an attack on the king, and the author was sentenced to have both of his ears cut off. It seems, however, that some parts of Prynne's ears were still attached following the procedure: after further controversial writing, particularly against bishops, the remaining parts were removed, and the author's two cheeks were branded with an 'S' and an 'L' respectively, the letters standing for 'Seditious Libeller'.

A famous witness of Prynne's second mutilation in 1637 was the aforementioned Leveller, John Lilburne. Henry Burton, one of the men being punished alongside Prynne, looked down at Lilburne and asked, 'Son, son, what is the matter you look so pale?'

Lilburne was an agitator for political and religious reform who was converted to Quakerism while in prison at Dover in 1655. His new faith was strengthened by reading tracts by James Nayler, sent to him from London. He was immensely impressed by these, saying they contained 'a great deal of the quickening life and power of the spirit of God'.

Although Lilburne embraced Quakerism,

Prynne wrote against the Quakers, for instance in his tract *The Quakers Unmask'd*, first published in 1655.

For offenders who were judged to have committed more serious crimes than Prynne's, the elaborate and grisly process of hanging, drawing and quartering was still in use as a method of execution.

Prisoners who were not executed, beaten, maimed or branded in the public streets could find themselves undergoing comparable punishments indoors, in prison. When the early Quaker Thomas Ellwood was taken to the Old Bridewell prison in London, he was shown a court-room with a dismal adjacent room, with black walls, where a whipping-post had been set up. He surmised that this en-suite arrangement had been established so that judges who sat in the court could sentence prisoners to a whipping, then witness their sentence being carried out straight away.

Although the whippings at Bridewell were not public, in that they were not deliberately staged in the open air in front of a crowd, spectators could come and watch on Wednesday and Friday mornings, when the whippings took place. Floggings of half-naked women were particularly popular, and in 1677 a gallery was built to accommodate larger audiences. Sometimes the whippings were not limited by a number of blows specified in the sentence, and would continue until the judge knocked with his gavel to stop them. Sir Thomas Middleton, a harsh judge and president of Bridewell in the early seventeenth century, often delayed knocking for so long that the spectators would cry out, 'Knock, Sir Thomas, knock!' He became associated with this phrase, so that Londoners would shout it at him if they saw him in the street.

Sometimes the punishments meted out to the early Quakers seem not to have had anything to do with a judicial sentence, but merely sprang from the sadistic minds of their jailers. Richard Sale, a Chester man who had become a Quaker in 1654, was often locked up in the city's Northgate Prison. There, the prison staff amused themselves by trying to stuff him into a hole in the wall called Little Ease. The Quaker historian William Braithwaite, whose 1912 book *The Beginnings of Quakerism* is still of great use to the researcher, described Sale as 'corpulent'. The business of pushing him into Little Ease was therefore so violent that 'the blood gushed from his mouth and nose', his body and legs swelled up, and he died as a direct result of this treatment, in 1677.

There was a similar hole, also called Little Ease, in the Tower of London, but this one was called a cell and had a proper lockable door, with its grim name on a plaque above. James

Parnell, traditionally recognised as the first martyr to die for his Quaker beliefs, was also put into two similar holes in the walls of Colchester Jail in Essex. The 'quaking boy', as he was called, was first placed in a hole so high up off the ground that he had to climb up a rope to get to it. He was not allowed to take food and drink up by a rope, and one day when he was trying to climb back up to his hole with his food, he fell onto the stone floor far below. He was then placed in another hole called the Oven, but died at the age of thirty after eight months under this harsh prison regime, in April 1656; the year of James Nayler's punishment.

The aforementioned English philosopher Thomas Hobbes, who lived right through the civil wars, is famous for supposedly saying that life is 'nasty, brutish and short'. In fact, in his book *Leviathan* (published in 1651) he said that 'the life of man' was 'solitary, poor, nasty, brutish and short' *in times of war and chaos*. Since Hobbes wrote his book during the civil wars, we can assume that this famous observation, so often taken out of its proper context, was based on experience as well as disinterested reflection.

If the treatment of Quakers and others who fell into the hands of the haphazard justice system of the time was harsh, many of the experiences of both soldiers and civilians who found themselves caught up in the civil wars and their aftermath were even harsher. The charge laid against King Charles I by his enemies in parliament – the charge that led to his execution in front of the Banqueting House in London in 1649 – includes mention of the 'treasons, murders, rapines, burnings, spoils, desolations, damages and mischiefs' of the war, in which more than eighty thousand people are thought to have died (a much higher number may also have died of diseases related to the war).

In the civil war armies, discipline was enforced by meting out punishments familiar to anyone who has studied the civilian justice system of the time. Sir Ralph Hopton, a royalist lieutenant-general, followed the motto 'pay well, command well, hang well' in his interactions with the men who served under him.

There were many sieges during the civil war, and if the enemy outside was determined to starve out the people inside the walls of the castle or city under siege, there could be great suffering for civilians. When the besiegers chose to take the place by storm, they would sometimes kill indiscriminately, as at Preston in Lancashire where the invaders killed 'all before them without any respect . . . killing, stripping and spoiling all they could meet with'.

After the 1645 battle of Naseby in

Northamptonshire the victorious parliamentary troops subjected the women of the royalist camp to barbarous treatment: those from Ireland were killed immediately, and the faces of the rest were slashed with daggers.

In 1649, the year of the king's execution, Cromwell led his most notorious siege, not of an English city, but of Drogheda, north of Dublin. Here, as many as four thousand civilians may have been killed. In a letter about the siege, the Lord Protector wrote that 'this is a righteous judgement of God upon these barbarous wretches'.

Since they could not rely on a steady flow of payment, the civil war soldiers would supplement their incomes by simple theft, and also widespread pillaging, after they had captured a fortified house, town or city. After the siege of Basing House, near Basingstoke in Hampshire, one soldier found himself with '120 pieces of gold for his share', while others got plate and jewels. After the sack of Dundee, General Monk's troops seized coins and valuables worth more than two hundred thousand pounds – worth over fifteen million pounds at today's values, or nineteenth million US dollars.

Towns that had been taken by enemy armies actually expected to be plundered, and sometimes the citizens would be prepared to pay a 'bounty' 'in lieu of plunder'. On a smaller scale, anything belonging to prisoners of war was regarded as 'lawful plunder'.

The conduct of war, and the harsh punishments meted out by the justice system, sometimes to people who had not committed anything that would be recognised as a crime at all today, are just two of the things that made Nayler's England very different from the same country today.

As the brutal response to Prynne's *Histriomastix* demonstrated, religion and politics were so thoroughly mixed in those days that the two were really identical. Many of Prynne's arguments against players and playing were drawn from Christian authors, yet his book was regarded as politically seditious. Whereas today political people might talk about socialism, communism, capitalism and libertarianism, British parliaments, political assemblies and political literature in the seventeenth century were obsessed with such religious 'isms' as Arminianism, Roman Catholicism and Calvinism. Religious affiliation seemed to be identical to political affiliation, and such issues as what we would now call defence policy, national identity, patriotism, loyalty and the rule of law were all bound up with religious faith.

Another feature of the seventeenth century that sets it apart from our own was the tendency of people to think not only in religious, but in specifically biblical terms. James Nayler himself was evidently extremely well-read in the Bible, and was able to quote from it fluently in his writing, and in the sometimes hostile verbal debates he engaged in, or was drawn into, with members of other Christian sects.

An example of the biblical thinking of the age: in condemning King Charles, the parliamentarians frequently referred to him as 'that man of blood', a reference to the second Old Testament book of Samuel:

Come out, come out, thou bloody man, and thou man of Belial

(2 Samuel 16:7)

It is in this part of the second book of Samuel that we come across Absalom, the rebellious son of King David. One of the masterpieces of English seventeenth-century literature is John Dryden's poem *Absalom and Achitophel,* which uses the Old Testament story to shed light on contemporary events in Britain. It is entirely typical of the age that one of its greatest poets looked for a biblical model to help him reflect on current affairs.

Another of the literary giants of the time, Dryden's older contemporary John Milton, based his *Paradise Lost* on the stories of the falls of Lucifer and of Adam and Eve. There is a link between the poet Milton and the aforementioned Quaker, Thomas Ellwood. As a blind man, Milton needed a secretary, and Ellwood served him in that capacity. The story goes that, following the success of *Paradise Lost*, Ellwood suggested that his master write the shorter sequel *Paradise Regained*, about Christ's temptation in the wilderness.

While Charles I was often insulted in biblical terms, his successor Oliver Cromwell was subjected to the same sort of name-calling after the king had been executed and Oliver had become Lord Protector. He was compared to the 'vile person' of the book of Daniel:

And in his estate shall stand up a vile person, to whom they shall not give the honour of the kingdom

(Daniel 11:21)

Another sign of the religious character of the age are the so-called 'field words' used by the parliamentary army during the civil war. These were necessary because, in those days before proper uniforms, combatants could sometimes find themselves accidentally fighting against someone who was actually on their side. This could easily happen, particularly when 'field signs', such as a strip of coloured cloth attached to a helmet, were lost in the heat of battle. Among Parliamentary field words were 'God with us', 'Jesus bless us' and even the word 'religion' itself.

At Thomas Fairfax's successful siege of Leeds in 1643, where James Nayler distinguished himself as a soldier, the watchword was 'Emmanuel', from the Hebrew for 'God with us'; and one Jonathan Scholefield of Todmorden in West Yorkshire recited the sixty-eighth psalm during an attack on the enemy's guns:

Let God arise, let his enemies be scattered: let them also that hate him flee before him. As smoke is driven away, so drive them away . . .

Todmorden was able to reach the enemy's guns because of a brave action by Nayler and others. In a 1643 pamphlet with a very long title beginning *The Rider of the White Horse* we learn that the royalist defenders of Leeds had placed cannon on a bridge over the river Aire. Fairfax's officers realised that if they could sneak a small force of men onto the river-side without attracting the attention of the sentries on the bridge, they would be able to hide in 'a little lane' and fire on the enemy positions across the river. The anonymous author of *The*

Rider of the White Horse describes Nayler as a 'dragooner', and says that he was the first man into the little lane. A demi-culverin (a medium-sized cannon) began to fire on Nayler and his comrades from the bridge, but their musket-fire caused the royalist sentries to flee, which made the royalist earthworks across the river much more vulnerable to attack.

Although the word 'dragoon' later came to mean a cavalryman, at this date, dragoons or dragooners were infantrymen who rode to battle on horseback.

In *Behemoth*, his book about 'the history of the causes of the civil wars of England', Thomas Hobbes included the Quakers among the sects who became 'enemies which arose against his majesty [meaning Charles I] from the private interpretation of the scripture, exposed to every man's scanning in his mother-tongue'. In other words, access to the Bible in English not only gave people ways to insult their leaders, but caused some of them to stir up even bigger trouble.

Having set out some of the dangers attendant on 'every man, nay, every boy and wench, that could read English' being able to read the Bible, Hobbes goes on to imply that restricting access to the Bible would be a good idea. To support this argument he cites Moses, who 'suffered no man to go up to it [Mount

Sinai] to hear God speak or gaze upon him, but such as he himself took with him'.

But by the time Hobbes's *Behemoth* was published in 1681, the biblical genie had long been out of the bottle, and biblical ideas were being applied to many aspects of public life.

Although the close relationship between religion and politics in England at this time made it very different from the same country today, it must be said that, in many parts of the world, the end of the twentieth and the opening of the twenty-first century have seen the growth of religion as a political force. In the Middle East, in countries like Iran, the religious authorities have wielded a great deal of power in the political sphere, and nations like Turkey, which was once officially a secular state, have had to contend with growing political influence from religious groups. Meanwhile religious movements have inspired wars, rebellions and terrorism, particularly in the Muslim world.

III. Farmer, Soldier, Preacher

James Nayler's punishment was enforced in 1656, one of the Interregnum years in Britain, when, for the first and last time in its history, England had no monarch, and was governed as a republic. Shortly after King Charles I stepped out of that window in London in 1649, he had been beheaded in front of a large crowd. His country would not become a monarchy again until 1660, the year of James Nayler's death, when Charles's son, Charles II, was invited back.

In 1656, Oliver Cromwell had been ruling as Lord Protector for three years: his first and second protectorates were signs that the infant republic, which could have evolved into something like a modern parliamentary democracy, could not shake off its origins in the British civil wars that took place between 1642 and 1651. The republican government continued to lapse into the condition of a military dictatorship.

Although he suffered under it, Nayler had played his own small part in putting this republican government into power.

He had joined the parliamentary army in 1643, by which time he would have been around twenty-five, and had been married to his wife Anne for four years. He had already fathered three daughters by Anne, and they had moved from James's birthplace of West Ardesley In Yorkshire, some twelve miles north to Wakefield. There Nayler was probably what was called a yeoman farmer, as his father may have been. This means that he owned or rented a farm or farms that he ran himself: depending on the size and profitability of his holdings, Nayler might have been a man of some means, or at least someone who did not rely directly on anyone else for his employment, accommodation or income.

In his book on life in seventeenth century England, Maurice Ashley gives a brief pen-portrait of the typical yeoman of the time. In terms of class, these men were somewhere between the gentlemen, and the cottagers or peasants. By definition, gentlemen had independent incomes and did not usually have to work at anything. The cottagers and peasants generally *had* to work on the land where they lived, or else they would lose both income and housing, and end up begging on the highways.

Ashley's typical yeoman was hard-working, involved in local politics, served in the local militia, was tough, respected himself, resented the gentry class who stood above him in the hierarchy, lived in a good but plain house, wore correspondingly good but plain clothes, liked his religion plain, and might be as voracious a reader as his pocket would allow. Ashley forgives himself for calling such men 'the backbone of England'. According to Ashley, such a man was also more likely to join the parliamentary army than the royalist army during the civil wars.

A twenty-first century historian, especially a female one, might pay more attention to the role of the wives of these yeomen than Ashley does, emphasising their part in keeping the skeleton of seventeenth-century England standing tall; but the fact is that we know very little of James Nayler's life before about 1650 when he became involved with the Quakers, and we know even less about Anne Nayler.

Nayler's yeoman status seems to have been part of his appeal as a religious speaker and a personality in general. Thomas Ellwood, looking back on his first encounter with James, wrote that 'what dropped from James Nayler had the greater force upon me, because he looked but like a plain simple countryman, having the appearance of a husbandman or a shepherd'.

It is interesting that Nayler should have joined the parliamentary army in 1643, the same year that his new home town of Wakefield was successfully besieged by that same army. According to an important article published by David Neelon in 2002, Nayler joined the parliamentary army the day before the siege of Wakefield, and may even have participated in the battle. Sometimes, it seems, more men joined the parliamentary forces than could be properly armed and trained in a hurry, and these raw recruits would quickly be deployed in battles as 'clubmen', armed with clubs, staffs, sticks and agricultural implements. According to Neelon, Nayler would probably have brought a horse along with him when he was recruited, which would immediately have put him outside of the ranks of the clubmen (Neelon's article *James Nayler in the English civil war* can be found in the journal *Quaker Studies*, volume 6, issue 1, 2002).

The siege of Wakefield was one of the many victories of the parliamentary army leader Thomas Fairfax (1612-1671) who was only some six years older than Nayler. The surname of the victor at Wakefield is one of those that is always associated with this horrendous period of British history, along with the names of King Charles I, Cromwell himself, Prince Rupert and John Lambert. Both Thomas and his father Ferdinando Fairfax were great assets to the parliamentary war-effort in the north, at a time when, in the early months of the war, the royalist troops often outclassed the parliamentarians on the battlefield. It was said of the Fairfaxes, father and son, that they had an 'inability to understand that they had been beaten'. Thomas was 'the man most beloved and relied upon by the rebels in the north', and at the battle of Winceby in Lincolnshire he cried, 'Come let us fall on; I never prospered better then when I fought against the enemy three or four to one'.

Fairfax's victorious siege of Wakefield was just one example of Thomas's reckless but lucky approach to warfare. Believing that the town was only occupied by a few hundred royalists, 'Black Tom', as he was called, started his attack, only to learn that there were more than three thousand of the enemy inside. He decided to press on, and took the town, capturing over fourteen hundred prisoners.

As we have seen, men of James Nayler's class were likely to side with the parliamentarians against the king: James may have joined up because he had an idealistic belief in the rightness of parliamentary government, as opposed to the rule of an absolute monarch.

We are tempted to assume that Nayler had some altruistic motive for becoming a soldier under Fairfax, since so many of his actions later in life were motivated by his beliefs. It is to be hoped that Nayler was not one of those mentioned in Hobbes's *Behemoth*, who longed for war because they had 'wasted their fortunes, or thought them too mean for the good parts they thought were in themselves; and more there were, that had able bodies, but saw no means how honestly to get their bread'.

If any comrades of Nayler's had joined up for the pay, they would have been disappointed. Parliament seldom paid its soldiers in full or on time, and later Thomas Fairfax was forced to mediate between parliament and the soldiers, who refused to disband until their masters coughed up what they had been promised. Nayler's later commanding officer, John Lambert, was also involved in the army's negotiations with parliament. Neelon reveals that Nayler himself sat on one of the army councils that represented the disgruntled troops at this time.

In defending parliament, many of Nayler's more thoughtful comrades may have believed that they were defending Protestantism against the Roman Catholicism some thought the king was trying to emulate with his unpopular 'Arminian' religious stance. Parliament generally favoured Calvinism, which was then seen by many as the opposite of Arminianism, with its emphasis on outward ceremonies. The

Calvinists tended to be Presbyterians, which meant that they wanted to organise the national church without the use of bishops. King Charles, like his father before him, wanted to keep the bishops: indeed, James I had believed that a national church without bishops was inconsistent with monarchy.

While parliament itself tended to favour Calvinism and Presbyterianism, the parliamentary army became a home for the Independent strand of English seventeenth-century religious thought. Many of the soldiers wanted to see a flourishing eco-system of self-governing, independent local churches, and Nayler himself was a member of such a church before he became a Quaker.

While many of the soldiers under Fairfax and the other parliamentary army leaders imagined they were fighting for a better religious and political system, many also tried to recreate the religious conditions they wanted to enjoy when the war was over, in the army itself. Religious cliques sprang up among the soldiers, and preachers emerged, one of these being James Nayler.

The Puritan preacher and writer Richard Baxter, who, as we shall see, faced Nayler in a duel of pamphlets years later, abandoned his church at Kidderminster for part of the war to serve as a chaplain under Colonel Edward

Whalley. His motivation for doing so was his belief that the country was seriously threatened by certain influential men in the army, who were 'proud, self-conceited, hot-headed sectaries' who 'by their very heat and activity bore down the rest and carried them along with them, and were the soul of the army'. Such men, in Baxter's view, 'took the king for a tyrant and an enemy, and really intended absolutely to master him or to ruin him'. Although he always suffered from poor health, Baxter risked his neck in the army in the hope that his teaching would bring these hot-heads, as he saw them, back to what he regarded as Christian orthodoxy.

After some seven years under Fairfax, Nayler became a quartermaster in John Lambert's cavalry.

Like both Nayler and Thomas Fairfax, Lambert was a Yorkshireman. Like Fairfax, he was a brave and gifted military commander, though he seems to have been more circumspect and less reckless in his approach to the battlefield.

Lambert's careful preparation and observation of the enemy's force underpinned the parliamentary victory at the Battle of Dunbar in 1650. By this time parliament was fighting the Scots, who themselves were fighting for King Charles II, whom they had declared King of Scotland and crowned at Scone. The Battle of Dunbar is important for the story of James Nayler because he was actually there, as he had been at Fairfax's siege of Leeds in 1643. But this time, Nayler was serving under Lambert.

Given the religious way of thinking of people at the time, it is hardly surprising that the battles of the civil wars called the infernal kingdom to their minds.

A parliamentary captain called the 1644 Battle of Marston Moor 'Hell's gates', and complained that during the battle he was both deafened by explosions and shouts, and blinded by smoke. Sometimes the smoke from guns and muskets blocked out the sun, so that the only light was the flashes from the mouths of these death-dealing devices, and comrades could not see each other, or the enemy, or even where they were. Neelon has revealed that James Nayler was at this hellish Battle of Marston Moor west of York, where over four thousand men lost their lives. By examining army records from the time, Neelon has determined that Nayler was probably also at the battles of Adwalton Moor near Bradford, Nantwich in Cheshire, at the siege of Pontefract in Yorkshire, and at some less important engagements.

Before the Battle of Dunbar in 1650, the Scots were confident that they had a weak, dispirited English army trapped and ready to surrender. In the wee small hours of the morning of the battle, they were ordered to get some rest, sheltering from the rain under haystacks. Later, part of the Scots army came down from their strong position on Doon Hill: this was the tactical blunder that Cromwell said was an example of the Lord delivering the enemy into his hands.

Unlike Thomas Fairfax, John Lambert, under whom Nayler served at Dunbar, was a formidable politician, seeming to know instinctively when to push for what he wanted, when to bide his time, and when to absent himself from the scene altogether, and spend his time tending his celebrated garden at Wimbledon. Later, Lambert would become one of the twelve major-generals Oliver Cromwell appointed to oversee the government of England and Wales. Lambert was supposed to be in charge of five counties in the north of England, including James Nayler's native Yorkshire, but because of his other duties, two deputies stood in his place. One of these was Robert Lilburne, the brother of the aforementioned radical John Lilburne.

Rather like Shakespeare's Coriolanus, Nayler's first commander Thomas Fairfax was thrust into politics by virtue of his military success, and like the eponymous hero of Shakespeare's play, Black Tom found himself quite out of his element. Lambert, by contrast, proved to be a natural leader both on the battlefield and in the committee room, and at times he seems to have been second only to Cromwell himself, able to influence Cromwell's decisions. For a time, he was even regarded as Oliver's natural successor. In the title of a biography written by W. H. Dawson and published in 1938, Lambert is described, with good cause, as 'Cromwell's understudy'.

Like Fairfax, Lambert spoke for the army in the corridors of power, insisting that they be paid in full before being made to disband, and pushing for a legal indemnity for the soldiers, which would mean that they could not be prosecuted for crimes they had committed during the war.

Lambert's concern for the army was part of his fairly discernible and consistent approach to politics: he wanted the army to have a say, he did not want a restoration of the monarchy, he was against Cromwell giving himself the title of king, he was suspicious of parliaments, and supportive of a wide range of religious opinions. He counted both Roman Catholics and Quakers among his friends, and the numbers of Quakers among his soldiers made some suspect that Lambert was a supporter of their religious and political aims.

It is entirely consistent with what we know of Lambert's views that he would have appointed a man like James Nayler (who was not, however, a Quaker at this time) to the important position of quartermaster. If Nayler held the high rank of regimental quartermaster under Lambert, his role would have been a very important one: a position of great trust, in charge of valuable resources.

As the name suggests, the quartermasters were officers who were responsible for finding lodgings or quarters for the troops when they were not actually fighting or marching. Quartermasters would typically ride ahead of the main body of troops (a risky business in itself) and arrange quarters.

The population of the whole of England at this time was roughly five and a half million, or about a ninth of what it is today. In some areas the people were thinly spread – this was very much the case in parts of Scotland and Ireland. In these wildernesses, the armies of the civil war might sleep in tents, or rows of improvised huts, but it was usually quicker, cheaper and easier to lodge the troops with the local population.

The armies on both sides of the war relied on 'free quarter' for accommodation, which meant that they commandeered the homes of local people, often very much against their will.

In return, the reluctant hosts would receive a ticket, which, in theory, they could exchange for payment at a later date. Since the soldiers themselves were seldom paid in full, it seems unlikely that many people would have received adequate recompense for their trouble.

Whereas in a tented camp, or among rows of rough huts, army discipline might have been easier to enforce, order could easily break down when the troops were scattered among the local houses and farm-buildings. From the point of view of the local population, particularly those of opposite or neutral political and religious opinions, the arrival of their unwanted guests must sometimes have seemed like the advent of a swarm of human locusts, commandeering (or just plain stealing) food, drink and anything else they needed, or liked the look of.

In his book *Cromwell's War Machine*, Keith Roberts mentions the case of a Scottish householder whose servants tried to stop the soldiers entering his house in the first place – but were soundly beaten for their pains. Once in, the soldiers drank six pints of ale at dinner. When the householder refused to top up their drinks again, they broke down the door of the room where the ale was kept. When the lady of the house tried to stop them helping themselves to more, they struck her with a pistol. They then 'sat up and sang, drinking until about midnight'.

Another reluctant host complained that 'a barrel of good beer trembles at the sight of' the soldiers, and that his whole house had been turned into 'a rendezvous of tobacco and spitting'.

Army life is often said to combine long periods of utter boredom with short periods of extreme danger. When not drinking, singing and striking their hostesses with pistols, the civil war armies would try their hands at poaching – and even kept dogs and 'fowling pieces' with them on campaign to assist them in this.

Poaching could be a feature of army life in a camp built from scratch in a field, but the problems arising from the soldiers acting like the world's worst guests were features of 'free quarter'. Properly organised, 'free quarter' need not have given rise to such problems, and it may be that John Lambert valued Quartermaster Nayler's contribution because he had the leadership and diplomatic skills to keep such problems to a minimum.

After the Battle of Dunbar in Scotland, Nayler was central to an incident that was recorded for posterity and has become part of the Nayler legend. The following anonymous eye-witness account, evidently from a parliamentary officer, was included in Quaker histories written in the eighteenth and nineteenth centuries:

61

After the battle of Dunbar, as I was riding in Scotland at the head of my troop, I observed, at some distance from the road, a crowd of people, and one higher than the rest; upon which I sent one of my men to see, and bring me word, what was the meaning of this gathering. And seeing him ride up and stay there, without returning according to my order, I sent a second, who stayed in like manner; and then I determined to go myself. When I came thither, I found it was James Nayler preaching to the people; but with such power and reaching energy, as I had not till then been witness of. I could not help staying a little, although I was afraid to stay; for I was made a Quaker, being forced to tremble at the sight of myself. I was struck with more terror by the preaching of James Nayler, than I was at the battle of Dunbar, when we had nothing else to expect, but to fall prey to the swords of our enemies, without being able to help ourselves.

It is easy to imagine how this scene would be handled in some wide-screen cinematic epic of Nayler's life.

The camera drifts over the smoke-shrouded bodies of hundreds of extras in period costume, pretending to be dead or dying. The sound-track combines desolate, funereal music with the sound of Nayler's voice, steadily growing louder. In the next shot, we see the face of the speaker, shiny with sweat and darkened with gun-smoke. In a reverse shot, we see the shocked faces of his listeners, mouths gaping as if to eat his words whole.

As cinema, the scene might work, but as history it remains rather mysterious. What exactly did Nayler say, to terrify his listeners so much; and in fact, what does any preacher with integrity say after such a battle? And who were 'the people' to whom he preached? (Note that our source calls them 'people' and not 'soldiers' or 'prisoners'.) Were Nayler's hearers civilian camp-followers of the armies, or local people who had come to see the battle, and perhaps to pick over the bodies of the dead for valuables?

After the battle, where perhaps as many as three thousand Scots were killed, some five thousand prisoners were marched south to Durham. Conditions on the march were appalling, and it is thought that as many as two thousand Scottish soldiers died on the way. Locked inside Durham's Norman cathedral, over a thousand more may have died, of cold and starvation. The fourteen hundred or so survivors were shipped off as indentured labourers to British colonies in America.

IV. Quaker by Convincement

Although commanders on both sides in the civil wars may have attributed their successes to their superior experience, cleverness, luck, or God's support for their cause, the work of quartermasters like James Nayler would have had a profound effect on the efficiency or otherwise of the armies.

A force that had slept poorly on Thursday night could hardly be expected to fight well on Friday morning, and as the war wore on, those in charge of quartering realised that attention to detail in camp or in lodgings was important.

Where tents or improvised huts were used, these had to be kept clean and aired, and could not be erected too close together. If overcrowded camps became foul, various diseases could arise, and we know that after the Battle of Dunbar the English released a large number of sick Scottish prisoners straight away, along with those Scots who had been injured in the battle.

James Nayler himself was forced to leave the parliamentary army in 1650 because of sickness – usually assumed to have been tuberculosis.

Although today we tend to regard TB as a disease of pitiful Victorian heroines, it is in fact a very ancient malady, and is still very much with us. It is likely that Nayler had the disease, but with no noticeable symptoms, even before he signed up for the parliamentary army in 1643, and that the stress and privations of military life brought the symptoms out. Alternatively, he may have caught tuberculosis due to prolonged close contact with carriers or sufferers in the army.

TB brings fever among its symptoms, and can drastically lower the energy levels of its victims. These symptoms can lead to days of a kind of confused depression, with contrasting periods of giddy optimism; and it is possible that TB fostered some of the curious emotional states that Nayler seems to have experienced. If he really had TB, and understood what he had, then the threat of death from the disease may have sharpened his awareness of mortality, and caused him to think deeply about the Christian hope of life after death.

Neelon suggests that pneumonia or even influenza may have been medical causes for Nayler's discharge from the army. He points out that James's last winter as a soldier, 1650-51 according to the modern calendar, was very harsh, combining extreme dampness and cold. It was hard for the troops to find adequate shelter or food, and as a result such large numbers died on both sides that reinforcements were needed before the war could be resumed in the spring.

After his time in the army, Nayler returned to the family farm, where it is possible that physical work in the open air reduced his tubercular symptoms, if he ever had any. He might have faded into total obscurity, had he not had a remarkable spiritual revelation while ploughing the land he owned or rented.

This incident is proof that Nayler's life was marked by a series of vivid, picturesque events, whether recalled by himself or others, all of which would be a gift to a screen-writer, or the author of a stage play about Nayler.

In Nayler's own words:

I was at the plough, meditating on the things of God, and suddenly I heard a Voice, saying unto me, Get thee out from thy kindred and from thy father's house. And I had a promise given in with it. Whereupon I did exceedingly rejoice, that I had heard the Voice of that God which I had professed from a child, but had never known him.

When he got home, he 'gave up my estate, cast out my money' and made an attempt to leave, as the voice had instructed him, but abandoned the scheme. According to his own account, soon 'the wrath of God was upon me' because of his failure to leave. He fell ill – so ill, in fact, that 'none thought I would have lived'.

As we shall see, Nayler's instinct that abandoning his property was the right thing to do on hearing such a call has a New Testament equivalent, in the instructions of Jesus to his disciples about how they should spread his message. It is also reminiscent of the behaviour of the fishermen Peter, Andrew, James and John, who abandoned their boats and nets on the Sea of Galilee and followed Jesus (e.g. Matthew 4, 18-22). There may also be a link to the advice of Jesus to the rich young man (Matthew 19, 21): 'If you want to be perfect, go, sell what you have and give to the poor, and you will have treasure in heaven; and come, follow Me'.

Nayler's story of an auditory hallucination followed by a sudden illness might suggest that he had caught a serious chill at the plough, and gone down with a fever, or experienced a flare-up of his TB; either of which might have made him delirious. But even if we embrace this medical, rather than spiritual, explanation, it is still telling that in his delirium Nayler should have heard what he identified as the voice of God, and not surreal, frivolous, familiar or demonic voices.

Before his revelatory experience at the plough, Nayler had already met George Fox, the founder of the Quakers, when that self-appointed and highly eccentric itinerant preacher visited the house of a Lieutenant Roper, who lived just north of Wakefield. According to Fox's own account of this meeting in his *Journal*, Nayler was 'convinced' there, 'convinced' being the Quaker equivalent to the word 'converted'.

But it seems that George Fox often thought that he had convinced people when he hadn't had such an effect on them, and the fact that Nayler needed God's voice as he worked at his plough before he succumbed, suggests that Nayler's 'convincement' was not all Fox's work.

In fact it was a while until Nayler took God's advice and got him out from his kindred and his father's house, but when he finally made the choice, his action was immediate, and innocent of any preparation.

In his own account, he suggests that he had made some preparation, but when he finally left home, whatever things he had laid aside for his journey were left behind:

I began to make some preparation, as apparel and other necessaries, not knowing whither I should go. But shortly afterward going agateward [towards the gate, or possibly road] with a friend from my own house, having on an old suit, without any money, having neither taken leave of wife or children, not thinking then of any journey, I was commanded to go into the west, not knowing whither I should go nor what I was to do there; but when I had been there a little while I had given me what I was to declare; and ever since I have remained, not knowing today what I was to do tomorrow.

Nayler's Call, as it is presented to us here, has clear biblical precursors. His inspiration that he should leave home with just the clothes he stood up in and 'declare' (meaning preach) may have been inspired by Jesus' instructions to his disciples as recorded in Luke 9, 3:

And he said unto them, Take nothing for your journey, neither staves, nor scrip [meaning a bag or wallet], neither bread, neither money; neither have two coats apiece.

In the version of these words of Jesus that we find in Matthew, he insists that the disciples take no money for their preaching, and should not prepare their sermons beforehand:

take no thought how or what ye shall speak: for it shall be given you in that same hour what ye shall speak. For it is not ye that speak, but the Spirit of your Father which speaketh in you.

(from Matthew, 19-20)

These principles of unpaid ministry and spontaneous preaching were and are central to Quaker ideas. One criticism the Quakers made of Richard Baxter, the celebrated vicar of Kidderminster, was that he prepared his sermons beforehand. To the Quakers, paid ministers like Baxter were, in Nayler's own words, 'hirelings: those that were sent of Christ never took tithes, nor ever sued any for wages'.

Although the second part of Nayler's Call reminds us of the gospels, the first part, where he is told by a voice to 'get thee out from thy kindred and from thy father's house' is decidedly Old Testament in character.

In Genesis 12, 1 God tells Abraham:

Get thee out of thy country, and from thy kindred, and from thy father's house, unto a land that I will shew thee: And I will make of thee a great nation, and I will bless thee, and make thy name great; and thou shalt be a blessing

This passage, which Nayler was surely referencing when he used the phrase 'get thee out from thy kindred and from thy father's house', hardly fits Nayler's circumstances at the time. He had already left his father's house and set himself up at Wakefield. Also, God was calling on Abraham (called 'Abram' at the time) to be a patriarch, found a nation and gain possession of land. As it transpired, Nayler was being called to accomplish a task closer to Jesus's task than Abraham's. Later, some would say that the Yorkshireman used Jesus as a role-model rather too enthusiastically.

The quotations from Nayler's own account of his Call printed above come from a record of a January 1653 hearing before magistrates at Appleby in Westmorland (now in Cumbria, a county that borders Scotland in the far North-West of England).

Nayler had been charged with blasphemy under the Blasphemy Act of 1650, an Act 'against several Atheistical, Blasphemous and Execrable Opinions, derogatory to the honour of God, and destructive to humane Society'. Among other things, the Act was designed to target any people who were not 'distracted in brain' but still claimed to be:

very God, or to be Infinite or Almighty, or in Honour, Excellency, Majesty and Power to be equal, and the same with the true God

This sort of belief – that one is oneself God – is associated in the 1650 Act with a related belief, that God is not as holy or righteous as the church claims. The Act also had punishments in store for people whose religious opinions led them to believe that 'unrighteousness in persons, or the acts of uncleanness, profane swearing, drunkenness, and the like filthiness and brutishness, are not unholy and forbidden in the Word of God'. The target here was the extreme Antinomians, who believed that, because they themselves were 'saved' or otherwise possessed some special, holy status, nothing they did could be counted criminal or immoral. To some in the British establishment at the time, these Antinomians, including the notorious Ranters, were spiritual descendants of the Anabaptists of sixteenth-century Münster, and were a serious threat to social order.

The unofficial leader of the Ranters (a sect whose very existence has been doubted by some historians) was Laurence Clarkson, a Lancashire man who came to be called the 'captain of the rant' and whose 1650 tract *A Single Eye* seems to have been one of the factors that persuaded parliament to create the Blasphemy Act of the same year. Like Nayler, Clarkson was tried for blasphemy, and was accused of sexual immorality, including following up the naked baptism of women by total immersion, with sex in the water.

The 1650 Blasphemy Act was much milder than its predecessor, the Blasphemy Ordinance of 1648. Whereas the 1650 Act provided for a six month jail sentence for a first offence, and banishment for a second, the 1648 Ordinance insisted on the death penalty, even for 'blasphemies' that were nothing like a serious as those targeted by the later Act. In England after 1648 and before 1650, it seems that in theory one could be executed merely for suggesting, for instance, that dead bodies would not rise again at the end of the world (the doctrine of 'the resurrection of the body') or that Jesus did not ascend bodily into heaven.

The 1648 Ordinance also lacked the 1650 Act's implication that the offences of people who blasphemed because of madness should not be brought to court.

Although it was clearly aimed at the Ranters, the 1650 Act was used as a stick to beat the Quakers, because lazy minds in positions of political power in England at the time tended to confuse the different sects. The magistrates at Appleby seem to have been concerned that Nayler was a prominent personality in an Antinomian group similar or identical to the Ranters, and that he might also have links with more politically-minded groups such as the Levellers and Diggers.

The Appleby magistrates tried to extract from Nayler exactly what he believed, and whether he felt that he personally was God or Jesus. This would not, of course, be the last time that James would be charged with, or questioned about, his supposed blasphemy. They also asked him about his background and his beliefs and practices: questions that were not all strictly relevant to the blasphemy charge. They also asked whether he had ever had anything to do with the Levellers.

Among the magistrates and others who questioned Nayler at Appleby in 1653 were Colonel Gervase Benson, who was already a Quaker himself, having been convinced by George Fox just a few months earlier. Also there was Judge Anthony Pearson, then known as 'a great persecutor of Friends', of whom more later.

The hearing began with an argument over Nayler's hat, which he refused to take off out of respect for the court. This is a custom, or, in Quaker language, a 'testimony' that many Quakers still maintain today; though in twenty-first century Britain hats are not worn nearly as much as they were in the seventeenth century: modern Friends will not usually have many opportunities to refuse to take off their hats as a sign of respect.

The refusal to give 'hat honour', as it was called, was something George Fox claimed was inspired in him by the Lord, who 'forbade me to put off my hat to any, high or low'. 'This made the sects and professions rage', said Fox in his *Journal*, 'the professions' here meaning not doctors, lawyers and the like but groups of people who professed a particular religious point of view. The general 'rage' this provoked against the Quakers led to 'blows, punchings, beatings, and imprisonment . . . some had their hats violently plucked off and thrown away . . . the bad language and evil usage [treatment] we received on this account is hard to be expressed'.

At the beginning of the Appleby hearing, Nayler explained that he refused to take off his hat not 'in contempt of authority', because he honoured the authority of God, but because he believed that this way of showing respect for people was against Scripture.

When Pearson demanded, 'Now authority commands thee to put off thy hat; what sayest thou to it?', Nayler replied coolly, 'Where God commands one thing, and man another, I am to obey God rather than man'.

The court having reached an *impasse* over the hat business, a Colonel Briggs began to question Nayler about his background. It was only after the accused had denied all personal connection to the Levellers that he told the story of his revelatory experience at the plough. Incredulous, Briggs asked, 'Didst thou hear that voice?', to which Nayler answered, 'Yea, I did hear it'. One is tempted to put the word 'hear' in Briggs's question into italics: a speaker of modern English might have asked, 'Did you actually *hear* that voice?'

When Nayler had finished telling the story of his convincement, Briggs, perhaps shaking his head, remarked, 'I never heard such a call as this, in our time'. Nayler's reply, 'I believe thee,' has a powerful resonance. One can imagine the court falling silent for a moment, as both questioners and questioned wondered at what had just been described. Later, Briggs called out to one Mr Coal, who was present, and asked, 'Did you e'er hear such a call as this? Did you hear it?' as if he were still shaking his head.

By using 'thee' instead of the more respectful 'you' when he said 'I believe thee' to Briggs, Nayler was reinforcing his attitude to doffing his hat. Like the French 'tu' today, 'thee' was customarily used only when talking to close friends, equals or inferiors; but the Quakers, some of whom still use 'thee' and 'thou', considered everyone to be equal. Later, Nayler would be bold enough to publish an open letter entitled *To Thee, Oliver Cromwell*.

At this point at Appleby, Judge Pearson tried to pull the proceedings around to the specific charge of blasphemy against Nayler, asking, 'Is Christ in thee?' Nayler replied that he could not deny it. Trying to get closer to the core of what Nayler believed, Pearson then asked him a series of questions by which he seems to have hoped to work out exactly what Nayler meant by 'Christ'. Nayler affirmed that he believed that the *spirit* of Christ was in him, since he 'filleth all places', but that he believed that Christ had been a man, and 'took upon him the seed of Abraham'.

There was nothing here that made Nayler guilty of blasphemy under the 1650 Act, so Pearson, perhaps wondering if Nayler had been arrested because of a misunderstanding, asked him, 'What difference then between the ministers and you?' Nayler explained that whereas the local ministers, such as one Higginson who was present at the hearing, believed that Jesus had been taken up into heaven in the body, he, Nayler, did not. He also asserted that he did not believe that the Jesus who appeared to the disciples after his crucifixion was Jesus in the body, but Jesus as a spirit. Since the first of these opinions denied the ascension, and the second went close to denying the resurrection, both of these positions would have been enough to have seen Nayler found guilty and executed under the 1648 Blasphemy Ordinance; but not under the 1650 Act.

Sensing, perhaps, that Nayler should not have been under arrest at all, and perhaps also feeling a little out of his depth in terms of theological knowledge, Pearson now stopped questioning Nayler, and Colonel Briggs started up again:

BRIGGS: Wast thou not of a kirk about Sawrby?

NAYLER: I was a member of an Independent church at Woodkirk.

BRIGGS: Wast thou not excommunicated for thy blasphemous opinions?

NAYLER: I know not what they have done since I came forth . . .

Pearson then resumed his questioning, challenging Nayler on the trembling and quaking of his fellow religionists. Nayler proved that this was scriptural, and the aforementioned Mr Coale chipped in with his own scriptural justifications, reminding everyone that, 'Moses trembled; for he saw the face of God'.

Pearson then questioned Nayler on the status of the Scriptures, and about the way he spoke against ordained priests. 'I speak against them that are hirelings,' claimed Nayler, ' . . . those that were sent of Christ never took tithes, nor sued for any wages . . . They are ministers of Christ who abide in the doctrine of Christ'.

Pearson then asked, reasonably, how we are supposed to know the true ministers of Christ from the false ones?

'By their fruits you shall know them,' said Nayler, paraphrasing Matthew 7, 16.

The account of the hearing that appeared later that year ends with Pearson saying, 'That is true.'

V. Fly as Thick as Moths

We know about James Nayler's examination at Appleby because of a short book of some forty pages that was published only a month after the event, in February 1653.

In *Print Culture and the Early Quakers*, Kate Peters identifies *Saul's Errand to Damascus* as the first 'proper' Quaker book, having the word 'Quakers' printed in capital letters on its title page, as part of its title.

Saul's Errand was also the first Quaker publication to be collected by George Thomason, who got hold of a copy in March 1653. The original manuscript was enclosed with a letter from Margaret Fell to her husband Thomas, who was then in London. In the letter, she asked Thomas to get the book printed, so that it 'may openly appear to the world what *[sic]* we live in'. It was printed for the aforementioned bookseller 'Giles Calvert, at the black Spread-Eagle, at the West-end of Paul's' (in those days, booksellers often acted as publishers as well). Calvert soon became the unofficial publisher-in-chief to the Quaker movement, publishing at least fourteen titles by Quaker authors in 1653 alone.

As well as publishing their books, Calvert allowed his house to become a makeshift post-office for the Friends, and even loaned money to Quakers who were newly arrived in London.

The vicinity of St Paul's cathedral in London (then the medieval cathedral, which burned down in 1666) had long been the classic place for booksellers in the capital: at that time, when many people were illiterate, and house-numbers were not used, business premises, and even some private houses, had to have pictorial signs, as English pubs do today; hence 'at the black Spread-Eagle'. In fact, one of the sights of London for visitors was the variety of interesting and colourful signs. In theory, the bottom edges of these signs had to be over nine feet high, so that a rider on a horse could pass under them safely.

'Lame Giles Calvert' lived above his shop in a tenement to the west of St Paul's, and was a prolific publisher not only of Quaker writings but of a range of literature, from radical controversial works to official government publications. Among the non-Quaker authors he published were the aforementioned 'Ranter' Laurence Clarkson, the Leveller John Lilburne, and the German mystic Jacob Boehme (1575-1624), thought to have been an inspiration for some of the early Friends.

The radical end of Calvert's stock-in-trade attracted criticism from more conservative commentators. Thomas Hall, a priest and schoolmaster from King's Norton near Birmingham, wrote that Calvert was selling 'soul poisons' and that his shop was a 'forge of the devil'.

Calvert's story got closest to James Nayler's when he published the Yorkshireman's books, and when in 1656 he signed a petition begging the authorities to remit the second day of Nayler's punishment in London. Martha Simmonds, one of the women who accompanied Nayler during the Bristol event, was Giles Calvert's sister: she was also the wife of the bookseller Thomas Simmonds, who published a number of Quaker books. Thomas was based at the Bull and Mouth at Aldersgate, which was then an important centre of operations for the Quakers in London.

Margaret Fell, mistress of Swarthmore Hall in Cumbria, who proposed the publication of *Saul's Errand*, was an early patron, supporter, organiser and protector of the Quakers. She married George Fox in 1669, her previous husband Thomas Fell having died in 1658.

The title of *Saul's Errand to Damascus,*

which was written by Fox, Nayler and others, reminds us of St Paul's original intention on setting off on his journey from Jerusalem to Damascus (see Acts 9, 1-22). In Damascus, he had intended to arrest any followers of Jesus he found in the synagogues, and 'bring them bound unto Jerusalem'.

The equivalents of Saul in *Saul's Errand* are 'some persons in Lancashire who call themselves Ministers of the Gospel, breathing out threatenings and slaughter against a peaceable and godly people there, by them nicknamed Quakers'. The book comprises several distinct parts, including the account of Nayler's examination at Appleby, and a piece called *Divers particulars of the persecutions of James Nayler by the priests of Westmorland.* It was these 'persecutions' by the local Anglican clergy and their followers that led to Nayler's imprisonment and examination at Appleby.

According to *Saul's Errand*, the first confrontation the local priests intended to force on Nayler and his companions started badly because two priests, some local magistrates and the mob they had assembled arrived too late to disrupt a meeting at one Widow Cock's house, about a mile from Kendal, an English market town on the edge of what is now the Lake District National Park.

As Nayler and co. were making their way

back to Kendal, the mob intercepted them, and one of the priests declared, 'Nayler, I have a message from the Lord Jesus Christ to thee'. He then went on to ask, 'by what power thou inflictest such punishment upon the bodies of creatures'.

This was a reference to the bizarre scenes that the enemies of the Quakers believed could be seen at some of their meetings, where many people were 'strangely wrought upon in their bodies and brought to fall, foam at the mouth, roar, and swell in their bellies'.

Nayler explained that these changes were brought about by the spirit of God. Then 'after much jangling' the priest said that Nayler, 'Taught people to burn their bibles, children to disobey their parents, wives their husbands, people to disobey the magistrates,' and much else.

Infected, perhaps, by the angry spirit of these words, some of the people present started fighting. 'These are thy Christians,' Nayler remarked, 'and this is the fruits of thy ministry'.

Nayler and his party continued over a bridge into the town, and stayed dry even though the mob threatened to throw them in:

But the raging people continued shouting, crying, and throwing stones at him, a quarter of a mile out of the town. But such was the power of the Lord that neither he nor any with him received any harm.

At Orton, a few miles to the north-east of Kendal, five priests, attended by 'many people from all quarters' called Nayler out of a house onto the town field. There they asked him about the source of his authority to preach, and reminded him of a parliamentary ordinance against preaching without authority. 'Paul received not his commission from man nor by man,' said Nayler, to which his opponents did not have an adequate answer; though it appears that they had a Bible with them.

A little later, Nayler put his own question, asking one of the priests present how he could prove himself to be a minister of the gospel, when he lived by tithes, which many Quakers at that time disapproved of, and refused to pay. To this, the priest so challenged had nothing to say.

After more attempts by the priests to trap Nayler with their questions, the people demanded that he speak, and he did so, while they 'gave audience and were very silent'. The priests 'had not one word to say against anything that [Nayler] had spoken'.

'Seeing there could be no peace there' Nayler and his companions tried to return to the house from which they had been summoned, but 'he and some other friends received stripes', meaning scars.

Saul's Errand tells us that the next Sunday,

the priests preached against Nayler and the Quakers, saying that 'the parliament had opened a gap for blasphemy' (in other words, the 1650 Act was not adequate) and that 'they did God good service that would knock [Nayler] down'.

On the Monday, an armed mob, with priests and a magistrate in attendance, stormed the house where Nayler was, and hauled him off into a field. There they struck off his hat with a pitchfork, and subjected him to more questions from the priests, while his loyal Quaker followers looked on.

'After much jangling and tempting', the priest who had been questioning Nayler still had not got 'the advantage he waited for', and fighting broke out again. Eventually Nayler was forced to follow the justice to 'an alehouse', running after the magistrate's horse. At last, he was thrown into prison because he would not take off his hat to his persecutors, because he used 'thou' to them, and because they called him 'a wandering person' or vagrant.

The next day, Nayler was taken to Appleby to wait to be examined at the next quarter-sessions.

As we have seen, Nayler's replies at his examination, where he gave the details of his original Call, were an example of his ability to answer questions, designed to tempt or trap him, in such a way that he was able to confound his critics.

At the examination at Appleby, Nayler did more that just confound Justice Pearson, who was perhaps his most aggressive questioner there. Anthony Pearson's old ideas about religion were turned upside-down by Nayler's words, and after a period of spiritual exploration, he was convinced of the truth of Quakerism, became an active Quaker, and was a powerful promoter and protector of the movement for many years.

Although only twenty-five when he first encountered Nayler, Pearson, a Lancashire man, was a justice in three counties, had been secretary to the parliamentary leader Sir Arthur Hesilrige, and had been clerk and registrar for the important Committee on Compounding with Delinquents. This body had the important job of, in effect, selling back to royalists lands that had been confiscated from them by parliament, because they had fought on the king's side in the civil wars.

Soon after Nayler's examination at Appleby, Pearson visited George Fox at Swarthmore Hall, the home of Thomas and Margaret Fell, which had become a kind of Quaker headquarters in the north (although, unlike his wife, Thomas Fell never became a Quaker himself).

At Swarthmore, Pearson found 'a family

walking in the fear of the Lord, conversing daily with Him, crucified to the world and living only to God'.

As a Quaker, Pearson travelled far and wide in the service of the society, was responsible for improving the organisation of the group, kept open house for Quaker preachers, wrote against tithes; but later regretted the early religious 'excesses' that 'made my carriage offensive to many', remarking that 'zeal in young years' commonly exceeds knowledge. According to Braithwaite, Pearson 'died a true son of the Church of England' around 1665.

Although there was really no legal justification for it, James Nayler was held in jail at Appleby until Easter 1653. As it is recorded in *Saul's Errand to Damascus*, the attempt by the priests and magistrates to frustrate the Quakers' missionary efforts in the north-west reads like a string of miscalculations. Trying to intimidate Nayler and his friends with large crowds of citizens armed with swords and agricultural implements, the priests and magistrates made themselves look like irresponsible thugs. Their attempts to confound Nayler with their supposedly superior learning ran aground on his plain, direct speaking and ready knowledge of the Bible. The examination at Appleby failed to find Nayler guilty of anything, his examiners were themselves confounded, and one of the magistrates was started on his route towards Quakerism just by hearing the prisoner.

According to *Saul's Errand*, Nayler himself seems to have realised almost immediately what a mistake the local big-wigs were making. Asked by what power he did what he was doing, Nayler asked, 'Dost thou remember who it was that did adjure Christ to tell if he were the Son of God and asked by what authority he did those things?'

This is a reference to the occasions recorded in the gospels when the Pharisees in particular tried to trap Jesus with their questions, call his authority into question, and tempt him to make outrageous claims. A good example can be found in Chapter eleven of Mark, where 'the chief priests, and the scribes, and the elders' ask Jesus 'By what authority doest thou these things?'

By asking his opponents if they remembered who had challenged Jesus in this way, Nayler was perhaps hinting that they were the modern equivalents of 'the chief priests, and the scribes, and the elders'; but he was also casting himself in the role of Jesus.

The fact that the local priests who tried to disrupt the activities of the Quakers are not mentioned by name in *Saul's Errand* makes them seem rather faceless and sinister, but in fact one of them, Francis Higginson, who was present at Nayler's Appleby examination and also at the Orton encounter, wrote his own account of events. His version, which is included in a piece called *A Brief Reply to some part of a very scurrilous and lying Pamphlet, called Saul's Errand to Damascus*, was published in 1653, and was the second part of a longer book, beginning with his *Brief Relation of the Irreligion of the Northern Quakers*.

According to Higginson, he saw no violence offered to the Quakers, though he heard of a regrettable incident where a young man tried and failed to trip Nayler up using his staff. Higginson also claimed that nobody on his side carried any weapons, except for two gentlemen who always carried swords, and someone who had brought a sword along because he was frightened of the Quakers, and wanted to be able to defend himself against them if need be.

Higginson also tells us that the priests did not bring a mob with them to the Orton encounter, but that a crowd of curious onlookers gathered when they saw that something was happening there. According to Higginson's account of the exchanges at Orton, and before the magistrates at Appleby, it was Nayler's opponents who won the day, and confounded Nayler; not the other way round.

Higginson is not a reliable source, because, like many Anglican priests of the time, he clearly felt threatened by the Quakers. If Friends' beliefs had really taken hold in England, Higginson and his peers would have lost their roles as mediators between God and the people, and interpreters of Scripture for their parishioners. If their priestly task had been taken over by a sect of wandering, self-educated preachers, most of whom were from a lower social class, the Anglican priests would have lost their status. Their lengthy, expensive educations gained at Oxford and Cambridge would have seemed pointless in retrospect, and they might have lost their incomes, and the vicarages and other church properties where they made their homes.

Though we cannot trust everything Higginson says, he does add some extra details to the story of Nayler's revelation at the plough which there is no reason to doubt. He tells us that this happened in 'barley-seed' time, meaning perhaps January, and that there were two people with Nayler as he stood at his plough, although neither of them heard the voice that called Nayler.

Higginson also tells us that when Nayler 'gave up [his] estate, [and] cast out [his] money', he did not give it to the poor, or share it out among his neighbours, but put it all into the hands of his wife. In his account of Nayler's examination at Appleby, Higginson has Colonel Briggs, one of Nayler's questioners, remarking, 'dost thou call that a giving away of thy estate, and casting out thy money? I should not much care if all my estate were so given away,' implying that by giving everything to his wife, Nayler was not really giving anything away at all.

It is likely that some farmer's wives at this period would find the business of taking on all of their husband's land a severe challenge, especially when that husband immediately absented himself, and there were no sons to help out with those aspects of farm work that were traditionally regarded as men's work (bearing in mind that the Naylers had three daughters and no sons). It is probable, however, that Anne Nayler took all this in her stride. She had, after all, probably been in charge of the farm during her husband's long absence during his military service. This is something that often happens in wartime: war being regarded as men's work, women are left to fill the men's places doing everything else, and often experience an increased degree of power and independence as a result.

Perhaps to dispel the impression that the authorities were 'raging' against the Quakers, Higginson's tone in his *Brief Reply* is often kindly and concerned. He puts many of the 'errors' of the Quakers down to ignorance, and says 'it is our prayer to the Lord for them, that they may yet . . . be clothed with those Christian graces, and filled with these gifts of the Spirit, which are ornaments of great price before God'.

It is interesting that in his *Brief Relation of the Irreligion of the Northern Quakers,* which precedes his *Brief Reply to . . . Saul's Errand to Damascus* Higginson quickly draws a comparison between the activities of the 'northern Quakers' and those of the Anabaptists of Münster. Once you have read his account of the Quakers, says Higginson:

. . . you will be ready to dream (if you be acquainted with the history of the last century) that you behold the turbulent exorcists of Germany, redivive [reborn] in England, and acting their old tragic parts over again, though on another stage

In his *Brief Relation*, Higginson is keen to show how the beliefs of the Quakers, spoken aloud by them and also recorded in their writings that 'fly as thick as moths up and down the country' not only revive those of the German Anabaptists, but also repeat the mistakes of other Christian 'heresies', such as Socinianism, Priscillianism, and the belief that it is possible for Christians to attain to spiritual perfection during their earthly lives.

The effect of Higginson's attempt to apply his knowledge of the history of Christian theology to his account of the Quakers calls to mind the common English phrases, 'there's nothing new under the sun' and 'we've seen it all before', both of which tend to be dismissive, and can be used to make new ideas seem old and worn-out.

The tone of Higginson's *Brief Relation* is not as mild as that of his *Brief Reply.* In the *Relation* he is clearly trying to alarm the reader, and like an irresponsible tabloid journalist of the twenty-first century he uses exaggeration, half-truths, hearsay and inflammatory language to make Nayler, Fox and their associates, whom he calls 'Satan's seeds-men' seem like a serious threat.

As well as indicating what he sees as the dangerously heretical nature of Quaker beliefs, Higginson gives an extremely lurid account of Quaker meetings for worship, where:

. . . though their speakings be a very chaos of words and errors, yet very often while they are speaking, so strange is the effect of them in their unblest followers, that many of them, sometimes men, but more frequently women and children fall into quaking fits. The manner of which is this; those in their assemblies that are taken with these fits, fall suddenly down, as it were in a swoon, as though they were surprised with an epilepsis, or apoplexy,and lie grovelling on the earth, and struggling as it were for life, and sometimes more quietly as though they were departing; while the agony of the fit is upon them their lips quiver, their flesh and joints tremble, their bellies swell as though blown up with wind, they foam at the mouth, and sometimes purge as if they had taken physic

Higginson is convinced that these 'fits' of the Quakers are cases of possession by the devil, and that 'George Fox, the ring-leader of this sect, hath been and is vehemently suspected to be a sorcerer'.

VI. Nayler and Richard Baxter

At the time of his confrontations with James Nayler, in the flesh and via the medium of the printed word, Francis Higginson was the vicar of Kirkby Stephen, a small market town in the historical county of Westmorland (now in Cumbria).

Although this whole area is known to the rest of the world as 'the Lakes' or 'the Lake District', Quakers with a sense of their own history call it 'the 1652 Country', after the year when Quakerism really began to establish itself. Although the pace of life in seventeenth-century England must have been much slower than it is almost anywhere in the world today, the progress of the Quakers during the years from 1652 was remarkably rapid. The sources tell stories of hundreds, even thousands of people coming over to the Quakers in a matter of a few weeks, for instance in London and Bristol. This is one reason why it is sometimes difficult to trace exactly what happened and when in early

Quaker history: it is always harder to take a successful snapshot of a rapidly-moving object.

Both Francis Higginson's father and his grandfather had been Church of England priests, which may have given him a keener sense of the potential Quaker threat to the religious *status quo* in England than might otherwise have been the case. His father was another Francis, who was an important pioneer minister in Massachusetts: in fact Francis junior had to return across the Atlantic to become a Westmorland minister, and critic of the Quakers.

Unlike his more famous father, little is known about the Francis Higginson who wrote against Nayler and other Quakers. This certainly cannot be said of another Church of England priest with whom Nayler came into conflict, in 1655.

In his book on Nayler, Leo Damrosch reminds us that, though readers who only see the Quaker side of the society's history may find all the actions of the early Quakers laudable, or at least understandable, yet from the point of view of the Friends' opponents, their activities must often have seemed alarming and threatening, or at least a nuisance.

Damrosch spares a thought for the poor struggling Anglican ministers who suddenly found their churches and vicarages besieged by mobs of excited sectaries, interrupting sermons, asking awkward questions, accusing them of all sorts of theological crimes, handing out challenging and inflammatory pamphlets, and luring away hitherto loyal parishioners.

An Anglican minister and author who was confronted in this way was the aforementioned Richard Baxter of Kidderminster in Worcestershire. Baxter was a well-known figure in his own time, and is still known, read and admired by many Christians, of many different denominations, all over the world today. Some of his writings, including *The Reformed Pastor*, *A Call to the Unconverted* and *The Saints' Everlasting Rest* are considered to be enduring Christian classics.

Among Baxter's later admirers was the nineteenth-century America Quaker poet John Greenleaf Whittier. Whittier included a potted biography of Baxter in his book *Old Portraits and Modern Sketches*. The book also includes biographies of the seventeenth-century English writers John Bunyan and Andrew Marvell, and the early Quakers Thomas Ellwood, and James Nayler himself.

Although he acknowledges that Baxter 'hated the Quakers' and that many of his writings 'are no longer read', Whittier asserts that some of Baxter's books 'can never become obsolete', 'belong to no time or sect' and 'speak the universal language of the wants and desires of the human soul'. Whittier makes it clear that among Baxter's obsolete writings are many of his 'controversial' works – those that, in Baxter's own words, were written in response to 'doctrinal controversies among Protestants'.

As to his character, Whittier says that although 'he had his faults and weaknesses, and committed grave errors', he was an honest man whose 'motives were the highest and best which can influence human action'.

As Whittier makes clear, Baxter certainly was not the kind of greedy, negligent Anglican priest the Quakers and other 'separatist' religious groups were trying to expose. He was incredibly hard-working, and simultaneously abstemious in his habits: so much so that his overwork and neglect of himself probably exacerbated his chronic ill-health.

Although chronic illness is not necessarily a sign of good character, Baxter's persistent and alarming physical symptoms have made some of his admirers conclude that his whole life was a kind of martyrdom. A similar idea has sometimes been applied to the life-stories of acknowledged Christian saints, especially those who did not die a martyr's death. These sometimes called 'confessors' because they confessed Christianity and lived by its tenets, but did not die for it. Among these are the saintly English king Edward the Confessor, and the Northumbrian saint, Cuthbert, both of whom suffered from chronic illnesses, though both are also supposed to have had the power to heal others.

The symptoms of Richard Baxter's chronic syndrome included 'incredible inflammations of stomach, bowels, back, sides, head, thighs, as if I had been daily fill'd with wind', and bleeding from 'eyes, and teeth, and jaws, and joints'.

In an ill-tempered little book called *The Quaker's Cathechism*, which James Nayler was called on to answer, Baxter addressed one objection that the Quakers made against him in a very revealing way. The Quakers criticised him on the grounds that he had never done any manual work – that he did not 'thresh and dig'. Baxter assured the Quakers that he would find the business of tilling the soil:

. . . incomparably a more easy life than that which I endure. Solomon knew, and I know to my sorrow, that much study is a weariness to the flesh; and might I but plough and dig I should yet hope to live in some competent health, who now spend my days in continual pain and languishing.

It may be that Baxter alluded to his sickness in *The Quaker's Cathechism* to make his Quaker opponents pity him. If this was his intention, then he must have been disappointed by

Nayler's response to the *Catechism*, which grants no quarter at all.

The life which Baxter endured included not just weary study, but also constant parish work, bringing the people of Kidderminster to Jesus. Baxter's combination of public preaching, personal counselling, catechising of parishioners, and collaboration with like-minded ministers, meant that he could say that: 'When I came thither first, there was about one family in a street that worshipped God and called on his name', but 'when I came away there were some streets where there was not past one family in the side of a street that did not so'.

Although his own health never seems to have been anywhere near good, Baxter's ministry to his parishioners included medical help: he combined the role of vicar with that of general practitioner. He met with notable success with patients suffering from 'melancholy' – broadly speaking, what we would now call depression. Baxter became so famous for this that all the melancholics for miles around would seek him out, looking for a cure.

Some of his contemporaries thought that Baxter himself was a melancholic, and given his work-load and his ever-ailing body, it is likely that if he was depressed, the mental symptoms were exacerbated by what we would now call stress. Characteristically, Baxter even wrote a book about this mental disorder, called *The Cure of Melancholy and Overmuch Sorrow, by Faith*.

Despite his prodigious output of written works, Baxter was not rich: he preferred not to be paid cash for his writings, and instead claimed a number of copies of his latest book, which he would then distribute free as part of his ministry. He spent much of his life lodging in other people's houses, married late, had no children, and spent ten years as a widower before he finally succumbed to his many maladies, at the age of seventy-six. It is ironic that this profoundly unhealthy man, who preached 'as a dying man' and was always expecting the Grim Reaper to visit him, should have lived to such an age, which was impressive in those days of wars, poor diet and rudimentary medical care. Baxter even outlived his much younger wife, who died in her forties.

Despite, or perhaps because of, Baxter's reputation as a highly effective Anglican minister, he and his church were troubled by the Quakers. The Friends disturbed a Sunday morning service, which was being taken by Baxter's assistant, because Baxter himself was then in his sick-bed. There was 'an unprofitable verbal discourse with an unreasonable railing fellow', after which the Quakers sent Baxter 'five several papers', four of them containing, in Baxter's own words, 'almost nothing but a bundle of filthy railing words ("thou serpent," "thou liar," "thou deceiver," "thou child of the devil," "thou cursed hypocrite," "thou dumb dog") with much more of the like'.

The fifth paper contained a number of theological questions, which the authors challenged Baxter to answer. Perhaps fearing the well-know power of Baxter's preaching, the Quakers insisted that he answer their queries in writing, and not during a visit to one of their assemblies.

Richard Baxter's response, *The Quakers' Cathechism*, which was published the year before Nayler's Bristol incident, is one of those controversial works of Baxter's that Whittier condemned as unread. The book is, however, important for the student of James Nayler, because of Nayler's reply to it, which was published in 1656.

One reason why 'controversial' works from this period can be a tough read is because the beginnings of the disputes reflected in the texts, as well as many of their details and their aftermaths, are sometimes lost to history. We have only a fairly vague idea of the nature and extent of Baxter's interaction with the Quakers before he wrote his *Quaker's Cathechism*, though we know from his autobiographical writings that he considered them to be an offshoot of the Ranters; that he believed them to be suffering from 'horrible delusions', and that 'many Franciscan friars and other papists have been proved to be disguised speakers in their assemblies'.

Unfortunately Baxter's *The Quaker's Catechism* is not the consistent, organised, systematic, thoroughgoing take-down of Quakerism that we might expect. Like both *Saul's Errand* and Higginson's replies to it, *The Quaker's Catechism* consists of several sections. These include an address to the reader, another to 'The separatists and Anabaptists of England', a letter to a young man who had fallen in with the Quakers, the testimony against the Quakers of a Bristol ironmonger called George Cowlishaw, and several sections comprising Baxter's answers to the questions put to him by Quakers. Baxter also includes his own questions to any Friends who might care to answer them.

There are repetitions and contradictions between, and even within, Baxter's sections: the author himself characterises the text as 'a few hasty lines', and its rambling nature makes it read like a rant provoked by Baxter's dislike for, and annoyance at, the Friends. Baxter himself admitted that *The Quaker's Cathechism* was 'but one or two day's work' and was 'no great interruption to my better labours'.

Baxter was a prolific and indefatigable speaker and writer on the religious subjects close to his heart – these subjects included his great theme of unity in the English church. He believed that the conflicting parties of Presbyterians, Independents, Calvinists, Arminians, Episcopalians and others, between some of whom there was already a great deal of overlap, should be able to cohabit happily inside a broad Anglican church.

Unfortunately, the quality of Baxter's written output did not always match its prodigious quantity: his faults as a writer are certainly evident in his *Quakers' Catechism*. Reflecting, in later life, on his written works in general, Baxter conceded 'that fewer well studied and polished had been better'.

The contradictions in his various utterances have meant that identifying what Baxter really stood for has proved a puzzle to many of his readers. One of his critics stated that 'Baxterianism' was 'a mere gallimaufry, hodgepodge divinity'.

Although he would like to have seen a wide range of shades of opinion included within the spectrum of Anglicanism, Baxter, like many who take a vaguely middle path, disliked the extremes that lay far off to his left and right. For him, these included both Quakerism and Roman Catholicism; and Baxter was not alone in suspecting that there was a hidden link between these two sects.

It would appear that Baxter included George Cowlishaw's testimony against the Quakers in his book because it included 'evidence' that the Quakers were in effect crypto-catholics. Cowlishaw swore that he had met an Irishman called Coppinger in his home town of Bristol, who was there making ready to cross over to his own country. Coppinger said that he was a Franciscan friar (though it is implied that he did not look like one, and was in 'mufti'), and that he had visited Quaker meetings in London. He had found that the Quakers' beliefs were 'near' to his own, and that they had 'approved' what he said when he spoke out in their meetings. He also found other Franciscans of his acquaintance, 'that were now become chief speakers among the Quakers'.

Coppinger told Cowlishaw that, though there were at that time no Quakers in Bristol, he knew that there soon would be – implying that he, Coppinger, was privy to a plan to send Quaker missionaries there.

Although, in his *Quaker's Catechism*, Baxter presents this fantastic story as if it were sensational new evidence against the Friends, the libel was old hat by the time Baxter repeated it: it had already been used by William Prynne in his tract *The Quakers Unmask'd*, and remained current for some time. As Bittle points out in his book on James Nayler, Quaker missionaries had first visited Bristol some time before this, in any case.

Baxter's inclusion of the Cowlishaw story is connected to what is the weakest part of his argument against Quakerism. Throughout *The Quakers' Cathechism*, Baxter repeats the accusation that the Quakers are in league with Franciscans and other Roman Catholic agents, who inform, encourage and direct their activities. Baxter claims (several times) that what he identifies as similarities between the beliefs of the Catholics and those of the Quakers make this supposed connection evident.

Like the people he called 'papists', the Quakers were, according to Baxter, hostile to the Anglican church, and resented paying the tithes that were meant to support that church. Like the 'papists', they also tended to down-play the importance of Scripture. Many embraced celibacy, which reminded Baxter of the Catholic monastic communities. Baxter also believed that the Quakers favoured English bibles over the original Hebrew and Greek versions, just as the Catholics supposedly preferred their Latin or Vulgate Bible. Baxter also touched on the Calvinist idea of predestination: the idea that an elect few are destined to be saved by God's grace, while the rest will perish in hell. Like the Catholics, the Quakers rejected this, believing that people can bring about their own salvation. This is not very explicit in Baxter's *Quaker's Cathechism*, probably because Baxter himself was not entirely convinced that predestination (a major theological bone of contention at the time) was as important as some of the stricter followers of Calvin claimed.

At one point, feeling perhaps that he may have over-stated the Catholic-Quaker link, Baxter suggests that it does not really matter if the pope or the devil inspired the Quakers. He does find time to remind his readers that the pope is Antichrist, and that the whole Catholic church is an instrument of the devil. By linking the Catholics and the Quakers, he is certainly not intending to compliment the latter.

Whereas Baxter's answer to the Quakers betrays his annoyance, James Nayler's answer to Richard Baxter is instinct with cold rage.

Somewhat longer than Baxter's *Quaker's Catechism*, Nayler's *An Answer to a Book Called The Quaker's Catechism* reveals much of its character in its sub-title: a very long sub-title, as was typical at this time, in this kind of literature:

Wherein the slanderer is searched, his questions answered, and his deceit discovered, whereby the simple have been deceived: and the popery proved in his own bosom, which he would cast upon the Quakers. Published for the sake of all who desire to come out of Babylon to the foundation of the true prophets and apostles, where Christ Jesus is the light and cornerstone; where God is building an habitation of righteousness and everlasting peace where the children of light do rest. Also some queries for the discovering the false grounds of the literal priesthood of these days, in the last time of Antichrist.

Although Baxter complained that the Quakers had insulted him with many 'filthy railing words', Nayler does not hesitate to continue to use hostile language against him, calling him 'a bloody persecutor', a blasphemer, a 'hireling', a 'dissembler', and a fool who tries to 'preserve [his] deeds of darkness undiscovered'.

It may be that if Nayler had ever got to know Baxter as an individual, he would not have written about him in this hostile way. There is a sense in the *Answer* that Nayler is merely applying to Baxter the standard insults the Quakers reserved for the ministers of the Church of England in general.

But Nayler had a particular charge to lay at Baxter's door, beyond the fact that the man from Kidderminster had written his *Quaker's Catechism* against the Friends. Responding to Baxter's accusation that the Quakers would not let him dispute with them in public, insisting instead on a written response, Nayler reminds him that the Quakers had previously encountered him during his public preaching at Worcester. According to Nayler's account, the Friends asked Baxter 'How the ministers of Christ and the ministers of Antichrist might be known?' Baxter's only response was to cry out something like, 'people, regard them not,' and then to stir up the people to 'hale them out'.

This reads like an account of a typical occasion when Quakers spoke after a sermon given by a Church of England priest. In those days, it was more acceptable to make comments, and question a priest, after the sermon. On this occasion at Worcester, Nayler tells us that a Quaker called Thomas Goodaire stayed in the congregation until Baxter had finished his sermon, in order to challenge him in this way, which was considered more acceptable than interrupting the sermon. Nayler tells us that 'all the satisfaction he got was that he was haled to prison: yea twice hath he been imprisoned by thy ministry'.

Nayler responds to Baxter's repeated charge that the Quakers are led by clandestine Roman Catholics simply by challenging Baxter to name the Catholics in question. He goes on to say that Baxter and his like are far more Roman Catholic than the Quakers, in that their church is little different from the Roman church that England broke away from under Henry VIII.

110

According to Nayler, the Quakers Baxter objects to possess a large measure of Christ's indwelling spirit, which gives them legitimacy as preachers, and guides them in everything they do. By contrast, Baxter and his like are led by the devil, and are only in it for the money: they abuse their power and cause their listeners (and readers) to become blind to the truth.

In later life, both Baxter and Nayler relaxed their extreme, aggressive positions, and even regretted the hostility they had both shown and provoked. Their hostility to each other's positions was born out of the prejudice of the times: like most kinds of prejudice, this sectarian strife involved characterising individuals and groups of people in crude and partial ways. It is possible that if the two men had met in Baxter's later years, when he had grown more mellow and loving, they would have found they had a great deal in common. But this was not to happen. When Nayler wrote his *Answer* to Richard Baxter, the Quaker had only four more years to live.

VII. Nayler and George Fox

As well as contributing their own pieces to *Saul's Errand to Damascus*, the first known printed Quaker publication, George Fox and James Nayler, whose relationship was severely damaged by the Bristol incident, collaborated in other ways before 1656.

Although, as we shall see, they were very different in many respects, the two men had plenty of things in common. In his 1994 biography of George Fox, *First Among Friends*, H. Larry Ingle revealed a curious link between Fox and Nayler that had to do with something that had happened in the previous century. It is possible that neither Fox nor Nayler actually knew anything about the connection.

Fox, who was born in 1624, the year King James I died, came from the village of Fenny Drayton (then called Drayton-in-the-Clay) in Leicestershire. In 1590, some nineteen years before George was born, Anthony Nutter, who had become rector of Fenny Drayton in 1582, was arrested because he was believed to be one of the leaders of the English Presbyterians. At that time, Fox's father Christopher (a pious man known as 'righteous Christer', who was later a church-warden) was probably deeply involved in the affairs of the village church.

Nutter's arrest happened during the reign of Elizabeth I. Earlier in 'Gloriana's' reign, in 1572, a group of Puritans had produced an *Admonition to Parliament*, calling for reforms to the English Church that would bring it more in line with what the authors thought Primitive Christianity was like. The *Admonition* targeted bishops in particular, and wanted to:

Take away the lordship, the loitering, the pomp, the idleness, and livings of bishops, but yet to employ them to such ends as they were in the old church appointed for. Let a lawful and a godly seigniory look that they preach, not quarterly or monthly, but continually: not for filthy lucre's sake but of a ready mind.

In the same year as the *Admonition*, the first English presbytery was founded, at Wandsworth. Soon groups of presbyteries were forming into 'classis' or alliances, which allowed Puritan clergy to have their own meetings. In these meetings it seems that extempore or spontaneous prayer was a feature – something that would later be embraced by the Quakers. The classis were seen as a threat to the Church of England system because their authority might come to challenge that of the bishops.

Anthony Nutter was arrested, with seventeen others, in 1590 because of his links with Presbyterianism; but Nutter's reforming spirit went beyond a mere preference for a system of church government that excluded bishops. He also got in trouble for such things as refusing to use the *Book of Common Prayer*, not kneeling to take the sacrament, not wearing a surplice, refusing to give the sacrament to an erring parishioner, and failing to uphold the ceremony of 'churching', which involved the blessing of women who had just given birth.

The cases of Nutter and his fellow-defendants were dismissed in 1590, but in January 1605 his continued refusal to conform led to his loss of the Fenny Drayton parish.

He moved some ninety miles north, to James Nayler's childhood home, West Ardesley, also known as Woodkirk, in Yorkshire. There he died in 1634, when James Nayler was about eighteen; and it is tempting to imagine that Nutter's thirst for reform, his insistence on plainer forms of worship, and his example of religious rebellion may have influenced Nayler; just as it may also have influenced the older generation at Nutter's old parish of Fenny

114

Drayton, where George Fox was born.

Even if no direct influence ever reached out to Nayler or Fox from Anthony Nutter, the fact that such religious rebels were active in the ministry in places like Leicestershire and Yorkshire in the early seventeenth century helps to fill in some of the background against which we must view figures like Fox and Nayler.

Although both held similar beliefs, and were influenced by a sense of dissatisfaction with the English Church (a dissatisfaction that had been pervasive for many years among certain groups of people) Fox and Nayler were also very different from each other in many important ways.

To begin with, the quantity and quality of the extant information about Fox and Nayler is very different. Fox died in 1691, in his late sixties, and he had time to write, and be written about, a great deal: he also collaborated with the aforementioned Thomas Ellwood on the compilation of his celebrated *Journal*, a classic Christian autobiography that gives a lot of detail about his life.

In Nayler's case, few of his writings are directly autobiographical, and many authors who wrote about him during his life were distinctly hostile and untrustworthy.

In England, social class has always been an important factor, but it is difficult to determine whether onlookers would have regarded Nayler and Fox as class equals, or whether one of them could have assumed superiority outside of the Quaker circle, inside which class was supposed to have no meaning. Nobody seems to know the extent of Nayler's land-holdings or those of his father, and it is difficult to judge to what extent 'righteous Christer' Fox, a prosperous weaver, was regarded as an important man in his community.

Nayler's social class was evidently a concern for the anti-Quaker writer John Deacon, who published his scornful *Exact History of the Life of James Nayler* in 1657. According to Deacon, 'some say he [Nayler] was a gentleman born and bred, others that he followed husbandry'. In his *Exact History*, Deacon goes on to say that his subject was the son of a sow-gelder, and practised the same profession himself until he joined the army.

Education is a classic way to advance to a higher social class, and the quality of Nayler's writing suggests that he may have received a rather better education than Fox.

In prose, this was an age of long sentences as well as very long titles. In *A Discovery of the First Wisdom from Beneath and the Second Wisdom from Above*, the book he wrote in Appleby prison in 1653, Nayler showed that he could manage those long sentences without losing touch with his meaning before the end, and descending into ambiguity or drivel. This assured writing style suggests a respectable degree of education in the writer, although ironically *A Discovery* teaches that wisdom gained from the outside world is inferior to the wisdom contained in the Scriptures that God has written on the human heart:

And abiding in that light it will show you a path which leads to purity and holiness, without which none shall ever see the Lord; and it will let you see a law written in your hearts, even the righteous law of the new covenant, which is a book sealed to all the wisdom of the world, and none can read it but by the pure light that gave it forth.

To give an example of another well-crafted sentence in *A Discovery*:

Now giving this up to be crucified makes way for that which is pure to arise and guide your minds up to God, there to wait for power and strength against whatever the light of God makes manifest to be evil, and so to cast it off, and so you shall see where your strength lies and who it is in you that works the will and the deed, and then you shall be brought into a possession of what you have but had a profession, and find the power of what you had but in words, which is hid from all professions in the world and is revealed no other way but by the pure light of God dwelling in you, and you in it.

117

Particularly striking is the way Nayler juxtaposes the words 'possession' and 'profession': what the reader once merely *professed*, he is implying, will now be *possessed* by him, because 'the pure light of God' is in him, and he is in it.

By contrast, George Fox's prose style is often direct and workmanlike, even telegraphic, so that it is sometimes necessary to re-read passages and guess at the words that George has missed out. One feels that Fox wrote as he spoke, and indeed many of his writings that have survived are known to have been dictated to amanuenses.

Whereas sentences from Nayler, like the ones above, are self-contained and can be understood outside of their context, it is more often necessary to have read a great deal of what precedes a sentence by Fox, to get the gist of what he means.

Addressing, in his *Journal*, a similar theological idea to the one handled by Nayler in the second passage above, Fox writes:

I had much discourse with the magistrates, wherein I laid open the fruits of their priests' preaching, and showed them how void they were of Christianity; and that, though they were such great professors (for they were Independents and Presbyterians) they were without the possession of that which they

118

professed.

John Deacon, author of the hostile *Exact History* of Nayler's life, claimed that his subject had no more education than might allow him to 'understand, write well and read his mother tongue,' but he suspected that the Quaker was trying to down-play his own education. Indeed, Deacon suggests that Nayler was actually a secret Jesuit, which, if true, would have meant that his learning would have stretched much further than a mere facility in English.

Deacon claims to know about Nayler and his Quaker comrades from public meetings at the Bull and Mouth inn in London, then the Quaker headquarters in the English capital. He also claims to have spoken to an old school-fellow of Nayler's who was then at Gray's Inn; suggesting that Nayler's school was good enough to have prepared at least one of its pupils for a future career in the law.

Whatever his subject's education, and despite his own negative feelings for Nayler and his sect, Deacon admits that James was 'a man of exceeding quick wit, and sharp apprehension, enriched with that commendable gift of good oratory with a very delightable melody in his utterance'.

Like many authors of pamphlets at the time, John Deacon's *Exact History* quickly runs out of material relating to its main subject, in this case the life and beliefs of James Nayler. Concerned, perhaps, that his piece might be too short to be worth printing, Deacon tacks on a series of lurid stories about the Quakers, including shocking tales of their going naked under the influence of the holy spirit. Deacon also alleges that the Quakers, including Nayler himself, are guilty of sexual misconduct, regularly going to bed with people to whom they are not married. Accusations of this sort were often levelled at Nayler and his Quaker comrades, both male and female. The fact that, in Quaker circles, men and women met together on a basis of spiritual equality seemed to provoke these accusations from religious opponents.

As we have seen, Nayler's 'convincement' came 'at the plough' when he was already in his thirties, had moved away from his parents' home, had his own farm, and a wife and three daughters, and had served as a soldier for nine years.

By contrast, Fox's Damascus moment came in 1643, when he was not yet twenty, was still living in Fenny Drayton, was unmarried, and apprenticed to a shoe-maker who also kept sheep. As described by Braithwaite, the decisive moment for Fox came at a fair when two of his friends, who were supposedly Puritans, tried to engage him in the familiar drinking exercise during which everyone toasts everyone else in the group. Apparently, this was a fairly new drinking-game at the time, having been imported from the Netherlands. The proposal on this occasion was that whoever drank least would pay the bar-bill at the end of the session. Not willing to join in, George Fox put down a groat (a coin worth four pence, or about two pounds at 2017 values) and walked out.

There followed a lonely night of mental torment for Fox, and it was in his own room that he heard a voice very like Nayler's, telling him 'Thou seest how young people go together into vanity, and old people into the earth: and thou must forsake all, both young and old, and keep out of all, and be as a stranger unto all'. One consequence of Fox's heeding that voice was that he soon left home to wander all over the country.

Unlike Nayler, when Fox was first challenged by the spirit he was still of an age to be a direct concern to his parents, who prevailed upon him to return home to Fenny Drayton, at least for a time. There he held long discussions with the local Anglican minister, Nathaniel Stephens, who, coincidentally, was a good friend and correspondent of the Kidderminster divine, Richard Baxter.

From the incident at the fair, to the voice in the night, to Fox's rejection of Stephens as a mentor, and his subsequent years of wandering and spiritual seeking, the story of the first Quaker's convincement is characterised by intense isolation. It is tempting to assume that the man was suffering from some mental illness at this time – perhaps a form of depression with a marked spiritual ingredient – and indeed depression, which as we know was called 'melancholy' in the seventeenth century, is certainly a condition that can make the sufferer want to shun society.

Although Nayler's convincement seems to have been an intensely personal experience, and indeed led him to leave 'his kindred' and his 'father's house', at least James had a pre-existing Quaker group to fall in with, whereas Fox had a lot of lonely wandering to do before he started to meet like-minded people who were prepared to accept him as a kind of modern prophet.

In this respect Nayler was more like St Paul, who received shelter and support from Ananias and other Christians at Damascus, after his experience on the road to that Syrian city had left him blind and helpless (Acts 9, 1-19).

It is unlikely that George Fox was right in claiming that Nayler was completely convinced by him during their first meeting, but nevertheless George must have recognised James as a useful addition to the Quaker ranks, at least at first.

The first mention of Nayler in many editions of Fox's *Journal* relates what happened in 1652 when the first Quaker visited a church (or 'steeple-house' as the Quakers called them) at Woodkirk near Wakefield where Nayler had been a member. This church was what Nayler's old commanding officer John Lambert would later call 'a very sweet society of an Independent church', but the congregation, led by a priest called Christopher Marshall, were far from sweet in their behaviour toward Fox.

Marshall who, like Francis Higginson, had spent time in Massachusetts, had also served with Nayler in the army. Fox tells us that:

When I came in, and the priest had done, the people called upon me to come up to the priest, which I did; but when I began to declare the Word of life to them, and to lay open the deceit of the priest, they rushed upon me suddenly, thrust me out at the other door, punching and beating me, and cried, "Let us have him to the stocks."

But the Lord's power restrained them, that they were not suffered to put me in.

Later, Marshall resorted to slandering Fox with accusations of witchcraft, including the use of magic potions, and bribery:

. . . as that I carried bottles with me, and made people drink of them, which made them follow me;

and that I rode upon a great black horse, and was seen in one country upon it in one hour, and at the same hour in another country threescore miles off; and that I would give a fellow money to follow me, when I was on my black horse. With these lies he fed his people, to make them think evil of the truth which I had declared amongst them. But by these lies he preached many of his hearers away from him; for I was then travelling on foot, and had no horse at that time; which the people generally knew.

(from Fox's *Journal*)

This alleged attempt by Marshall to make Fox appear like some kind of seventeenth-century warlock shows either his credulity, or the credulity and superstitiousness of his parishioners (which he was trying to exploit) or both. It is interesting to reflect that Marshall had been in Massachusetts, where, in Salem in the 1690s, the notorious witch trials were to take place: these resulted in the executions of twenty people. Closer to home, in 1612, the Pendle witches had been tried: they all came from the area around Pendle Hill in Lancashire, where George Fox had a spiritual vision or 'opening' in 1652. After their trial at York, ten of these unfortunate women were hanged. In the 1650s, accusations of witchcraft could still have very serious consequences. Janet Horne, the last person to be executed for witchcraft in the British Isles, was burned alive in Scotland in

1727.

It is implied that Fox visited Nayler's old church at Woodkirk alone, but he suffered similar treatment during a trip to Walney Island off the coast of Cumbria when he was with both James Nayler and James Lancaster, the latter a Quaker farmer who lived on the island.

The day before Fox visited Walney, where he had been at least once before, a local man on the mainland opposite the island attempted to shoot him with a pistol. Mercifully, the guns of the time were extremely unreliable, and though the gunman 'snapped' his pistol at George, it didn't go off.

Today Walney Island is reached via the Walney Bridge, which carries the A590 across the narrow strip of water that separates it from the mainland. When Fox and Nayler reached the island by boat, they were immediately attacked by 'about forty men with staves, clubs, and fishing-poles'.

These islanders proceeded to punch and beat Fox, and then push him into the sea. As he tried to climb back up onto the beach, they beat him again, temporarily knocking him out.

There was at least one woman with the forty brave men of Walney, because when Fox woke up he found that James Lancaster's wife was throwing stones at him. Lancaster himself was lying on top of Fox, trying to protect him from the missiles. It seems that Mrs Lancaster, who had perhaps heard or read the stories of Fox being a witch, believed that Fox had her husband under a spell, to force him to embrace the Quaker way. The forty brave men, it seems, had promised Lancaster's wife that they would kill Fox if he dared to return to the island.

When Fox got up again, he was beaten again, and thrown back into his boat. Lancaster then got into the boat with him, and pushed it back out into the water. Meanwhile their attackers continued to throw stones at them, and tried to catch the boat with their long poles.

But they had left James Nayler on the shore, and when they found that the boat was out of their reach, the mob turned on the Yorkshireman.

Fox and Lancaster returned to the mainland, where they found another mob of locals who were ready to kill them. Bruised all over, Fox walked three miles to the house of Thomas Hutton, a Friend, where he found he could barely speak, but he begged the occupants to go and rescue Nayler.

VIII. Ploughing and Sowing

After the alarming events at Walney Island, the remaining references to James Nayler in many editions of George Fox's *Journal* reflect a growing distance between the two men, who had shared such dangers together.

Shortly before the Bristol incident, Fox was taking his leave of Nayler in London when 'a fear struck me concerning him', though Fox does not tell us exactly what his fear was. This is an example of Fox's power of prophecy, which is sometimes mentioned in his *Journal*. In one place, he reports that while he was in prison in Lancaster Castle he had a vision that convinced him that 'the Turk', meaning the forces of Islam, would not in fact overrun Christendom; something that it seems many feared would happen around that time.

Also at Lancaster, Fox saw 'the angel of the Lord with a glittering drawn sword stretched southward', which he took to be a foreshadowing of the later wars with Holland, the Great Plague of 1665, and the Fire of London in the following year.

Fox's account of Nayler in his *Journal* ends with the words 'he came to see his out-going, and to condemn it; and after some time he returned to Truth again; as in the printed relation of his repentance, condemnation, and recovery may be more fully seen'. This demonstrates that Fox's feelings about Nayler's later Bristol 'sign', and the behaviour and ideas of himself and his close followers at this time, were extremely negative. Nayler 'had run out into imaginations, and a company with him, who raised a great darkness in the nation'.

Three years earlier, after his release from imprisonment at Appleby at Easter 1653, Nayler had resumed his busy schedule of travelling around, particularly in the north of England, preaching, holding meetings, visiting Friends and, in particular, writing.

From Easter 1653 to the Bristol event on Friday the twenty-fourth of October 1656, James was in great demand as a speaker and writer in the Quaker cause. He was often in the company of Gervase Benson and Anthony Pearson. Both of these men had been present at his examination at Appleby – as we know, Benson was already a Quaker at that time, and Pearson started to be convinced as he listened to Nayler there.

There is a sense in the records that Nayler was sometimes being drafted in to convince important or difficult groups or individuals, or to re-convince people who had lost touch with the reasons for their original convincement. The evidence for Nayler's regular deployment as a soldier in the pamphlet wars of the time is of course more solid than evidence drawn from, for instance, stories of meetings and other opportunities for preaching that are related by Quakers, non-Quakers or anti-Quakers. We have already seen how Nayler's writing talents were employed against Richard Baxter in 1655, and how Higginson responded to *Saul's Errand to Damascus*, which was written by Nayler, Fox and others: a great deal of Nayler's writing provoked, or was a response to, anti-Quaker pamphlets written by various individuals.

According to Kate Peters, in 1656 alone Nayler had a part in more than ten different pamphlet disputes, and between 1652 and 1656 he wrote approximately half of the warring pamphlets put out by Friends. He was writing at a time of increasing output from Quaker authors. Having published only twenty-eight pieces in 1653, the Friends published more than double that amount in 1654, and about a hundred items in 1655.

When writing was not appropriate, Nayler would oblige with a visit, or personal appearance. A problem among the early

Quakers that Nayler volunteered to try to deal with, or was called in for, was that of Rice (or Rhys) Jones and the so-called 'Proud Quakers' of Nottingham.

Like James Nayler, Jones had been a soldier in the civil wars, but unlike Nayler he had previously been a Baptist, and not an Independent, in his religious affiliation. Jones, his associate John Trentham of Mansfield, and their followers split off from the mainstream Quakerism of George Fox. The group were called 'Proud Quakers', or the 'Castle Company' because they held meetings in the castle yard at Nottingham.

The Rice Jones group had been convinced by George Fox himself. Fox had found these lapsed Baptists playing shovel-board, an ancestor of the popular British game shove ha'penny, on a Sunday; but soon they became 'Children of Light', as the Quakers were called in those early days.

According to the book *London Friends' Meetings* by William Beck and Frederick Ball, many of the early Quakers, in London and elsewhere, had once been Baptists. The isolation of the Baptist churches, which had no umbrella organisation to offer them national support, and their tendency to fracture over theological disagreements, made some of their members particularly susceptible to the new

Quaker gospel. In the case of Rice Jones's Nottingham Baptists, it would seem that the characteristic independence of the little church had made it possible for it to be dominated by one man.

Later Jones, whom Braithwaite calls 'a man of unstable character' seems to have inspired the Castle Company to try to be Quakers inwardly, without bothering with the outward 'testimonies' or ways of living that the mainstream Quakers espoused. In effect, they tried to kick away the Puritan underpinnings of the Quaker approach. Soon Jones was swearing (using profanities and taking formal oaths, which mainstream Quakers rejected) and arguing with George Fox over theology. Later, Rice's followers became 'the greatest football players and wrestlers in the country'; he opened an alehouse, and his associate John Trentham became an alcoholic.

James Nayler was not the only Friend to try to reason with the Proud Quakers. George Fox, Richard Hubberthorne and George Whitehead (of whom more later) also tried. Nayler found that in 'the things of God he [Rice Jones] is exceeding dark'; that he spoke in a confused way, and swore, using the word 'marry', a way of swearing by Mary, the mother of Jesus.

Thanks to the efforts of Fox, Nayler and others, by late 1653 Quakerism was beginning to be properly established in many parts of the north of England, including the north of Lancashire, the historic counties of Cumberland and Westmorland, County Durham, and Nayler's native Yorkshire.

Since, then as now, there was a higher concentration of people in and around London, the English capital became the next target for Quaker missionaries.

In those days, London's skyline was dominated by Old St Paul's, the church that would be replaced by Christopher Wren's masterpiece after the 1666 Fire of London. As we have seen, Old St Paul's was surrounded by stationers, book-sellers and printers. Other buildings that stood out from the capital's crowd of low-level structures were the Tower of London, the Banqueting House in Whitehall (outside which Charles I had been executed in 1649), Westminster Abbey and the Palace of Westminster. The latter was dominated by the medieval chapel of St Stephen, now long gone, which was the debating chamber of the House of Commons in Nayler's time.

With a population of around three hundred thousand, or over six percent of the population of England at the time, London then was similar in size to the modern cities of Hull in England, or Newark, New Jersey in the United States. It was, however, the third largest city in Europe, after Paris and Constantinople.

The city retained roughly the same layout as it had had in Roman times, and the narrow streets and alleys were often congested by too many pedestrians, horses, carts, and numbers of animals, including cows, sheep, geese and even turkeys, being walked into town to be slaughtered, butchered and fed to the population.

Old London Bridge, which was lined with shops and houses, was the only way to cross the river without taking a ferry, and it was often severely congested. The bridge, with its many closely-spaced piers, tended to slow down the Thames so that, in that time of the Little Ice-Age, the river would often freeze over in winter, and the famous frost-fairs could be held.

Most of London's streets were unpaved, and more or less permanently filthy, with stinking gutters running down their centres. The smell was supplemented by fires and the pollution from industrial premises, because London was then the country's biggest manufacturing centre. Among the more smelly businesses were those of the tanners and the dyers. As well as being a kind of factory town, London was also England's biggest port, and the centre of government and the legal system.

Although the sheer smell, at certain times of the year, must have been enough to put many visitors off the English capital, many Puritans, and some from the ranks of the Quakers themselves, felt that they could detect other evidence that 'something was rotten' in the state of London.

In a single-page 1654 tract with a title beginning *A warning to all in this proud city called London* George Fox told Londoners that 'your pride stinks before the Lord' and that 'pride and hard-heartedness abounds, cruelty and oppression grows and abounds in your streets'. According to Fox, Londoners were guilty of 'whoredom', 'all excess', 'lusts, and filthiness' and 'hypocrisy and dissembling'. They wore colourful 'changeable suits of apparel' and ate 'dainty dishes', and could therefore expect punishments from an angry God, including plagues and fire.

The 'apparel' of Londoners was also the target of Fox's particular scorn in his *Journal*:

What a world is this . . . women plaiting the hair, men and women powdering it, making their backs look like bags of meal . . . If he have store of ribbons hanging about his waist, and at his knees, and in his hat of divers colours, red or white or black or yellow, and his hair be powdered, then he is a brave man, then he is accepted . . .

Like much else that George Fox and the early Quakers thought, did and wrote, Fox's reservations about the dress of Londoners had a biblical precedent. In the aforementioned first letter to Timothy in the New Testament, women are advised to 'adorn themselves in modest apparel, with shamefacedness and sobriety; not with broided *[sic]* hair, or gold, or pearls, or costly array' (1 Timothy 2: 9).

Fox was not the only one to be struck by the colourful fashion-sense of the Londoners. John Evelyn, the celebrated diarist, noted that many women had started to wear make-up, although this was supposed to be an era dominated by Puritan plainness. Previously, only prostitutes had resorted to face-paint.

Although Fox witnessed what we might call decadence in action in London, this was the capital of an England that had got rid of its king and royal court, where Puritans now had a lot of political power, and where John Barkstead, deputy to one of the unpopular major-generals Cromwell appointed to control England and Wales, would soon be trying to curb the perceived vices of Londoners.

Barkstead's reign over the capital only lasted for a short time during 1655 and 1656, but it was another sign that Cromwell's government was in effect a military dictatorship, with unpopular Puritan trappings. Barkstead, the son of a London goldsmith, and once an officer in the parliamentary army, ordered the arrest of hundreds of 'loose wenches' and prostitutes. He also insisted on the suppression of annual festivals and open-air sports, the confiscation of horses used for racing, and the closure of the bear-garden at Bankside, just south of the Thames. This was where Londoners were once edified by watching dogs attacking chained bears, and where cock-fights would also attract enthusiastic audiences. Barkstead ordered the destruction of every animal in the place.

Barkstead's heavy-handed attempt to impose 'godly rule' seems to have been more effective than the efforts made by other major-generals and their deputies outside the capital. It may be that Barkstead could throw his weight around in this way because he was able to call on the assistance of some of the thousands of soldiers then garrisoned in London, whose visible presence on every street-corner was a feature of life in the capital at this time.

The London theatres, some of which were situated near the bear-garden, had been closed down at the start of the civil wars, in 1642. The city's taste for plays was such, however, that secret performances still took place; and William Davenant, rumoured to be a son William Shakespeare conceived with the help of another man's wife, took advantage of the toleration of musical entertainments to openly present his so-called 'opera', *The Siege of*

Rhodes, in London in 1656, the year of Nayler's downfall.

In a letter, the well-travelled Anthony Pearson warned Fox about how the character of the Londoners might affect the reception of the Quaker message in the capital:

for there are so many mighty in wisdom to oppose and gainsay that weak ones will suffer the truth to be trampled on; and there are so many rude savage apprentices and young people and Ranters that nothing but the power of the Lord can chain them.

It is interesting that, in his letter to Fox, Pearson does not recommend sending the most highly educated Quaker missionaries to London, to answer the challenge posed by Londoners 'mighty in wisdom', but rather those 'who dwell in the living power of God'. He implies that only these will remain unshaken in their purpose. Indeed, it would have been hard to assemble many very erudite Quakers in those early days. In any case, it turned out that the natural, rustic eloquence of the northern visitors worked well to melt the hard hearts of the sophisticated city folk.

Neither James Nayler nor George Fox were personally involved in the early work of the Quaker missionaries in London. The ground was prepared for them by various lesser-known figures, including young Edward Burrough, a remarkable early Friend whose preaching career contrasted in a marked manner with that of James Nayler.

Born at Underbarrow, near Kendal, in 1633, Burrough was seventeen years younger than Nayler, and not much more than twenty years of age when the Quakers began to make inroads into the London sects. Like Nayler, Burrough was the son of a farmer: his father James Burrough was a staunch adherent of the Church of England, and both parents disowned Edward, at least for a while, when he became a Quaker.

Like George Fox, Edward Burrough had begun wandering about listening to sermons and attending churches outside his parents' denomination, though in Edward's case it seems that he began his spiritual seeking at the very tender age of twelve. Whereas Fox heard a religious call during a sleepless night at home, and Nayler was called while he worked at the plough, Burrough repeatedly heard a voice when he was praying, when he was only seventeen years old. The voice said, 'Thou art ignorant of God – thou knowest not where he is; to what purpose is thy prayer?'

In 1652 George Fox came to Underbarrow, and met Edward Burrough, who was quickly convinced. 'I betook myself,' Burrough later wrote, 'to the company of a poor, despised and condemned people, called Quakers.'

Like the members of Nayler's old congregation near Wakefield, the people of Underbarrow entertained strange, suspicious notions about Fox. Seeing that he had run a long way from a tavern where they had recently seen him, they decided that he must have concealed wings, and tried to cancel a meeting with him that was scheduled for the next day. In fact, the first Quaker had merely run a short distance to give money to some beggars. When the planned meeting eventually happened, in a nearby chapel, Fox met with such success that 'after awhile the priest fled away'.

The early Quaker missionaries travelled around in pairs, a sensible practice which again had its roots in the New Testament – at Luke 10: 1 we are told that Jesus sent out seventy of his followers 'two and two into every city and place'. Even the number of early Quaker travellers in the ministry resembles Jesus's seventy – Quaker histories include Nayler, Burrough and others among the 'valiant sixty' who were the 'first publishers of truth'.

In London, Quaker pioneers like Burrough and his older companion Francis Howgill, who had been an Anglican priest, took every opportunity to preach and debate their message. It seems that at that time of political and religious uncertainty, Londoners would often attend formal debates and less formal discussion groups of various sizes, where religious issues could be chewed over. Since religious services held by different sects could turn into something like debates when members of the congregation, or visitors, stood up to speak, there were plenty of opportunities for Howgill, Burrough and others to air their ideas.

At first, many resisted their message: Beck and Ball put it well in their book *London Friends' Meetings*:

No doubt the London citizen, accustomed to the pulpit eloquence of learned divines, or the practised perorations of the teachers and expounders of those days, regarded at first these simple dalesmen with their provincial dialect as but the 'setters forth of some new notions' among the many such then prevailing . . . Yet this prejudice soon gave way before the wisdom and fervid zeal with which they spoke . . .

Burrough in particular possessed rather more than just 'wisdom and fervid zeal': he had a loud, commanding voice and an ability to adapt what he said to the concerns of his hearers. These qualities were invaluable in some of the noisier gatherings where he managed to make himself heard.

Writing about Burrough in 1712, the Quaker William Crouch recalled how:

In the midst of all which noise and contention, this

servant of the Lord hath stood upon a bench, with his Bible in his hand, for he generally carried one about him, speaking to the people with great authority . . .

The noisy meeting Crouch was describing happened at the Bull and Mouth inn in London' Aldersgate area, a building which the Quakers bought so that they would have somewhere to hold their larger meetings. There was a room at the Bull and Mouth which could hold as many as a thousand people (presumably standing up), but the fact that this was now Quaker territory did not prevent the meetings there from becoming loud and chaotic. Crouch recalls times at the ancient coaching inn when:

the room, which was very large, hath been filled with people, many of whom have been in uproars, contending one with another, some exclaiming against the Quakers, accusing and charging them with heresy, blasphemy, sedition, and whatnot; that they were deceivers, and deluded the people, that they denied the Holy Scriptures, and the resurrection: others endeavouring to vindicate them, and speaking of them more favourably . . .

Through the work of people like Burrough, Howgill and, a little later, James Nayler, many people in these chaotic gatherings were convinced, and it became necessary to set up separate, much quieter meetings where the new

Quaker converts could commune in a much calmer atmosphere.

IX. Signs of Stress

The Quaker pioneers in London – people like Edward Burrough and Francis Howgill – were keen to see leading Quakers from the north and midlands, like George Fox and James Nayler, preaching in the capital.

One possible reason why the London Quaker leaders wanted reinforcements was because they themselves were feeling overstretched. They were facing enormous pressures: they not only had to cope with large, noisy assemblies, which included many people who were hostile to Quakerism. They also had to contend with direct physical attacks, with the ever-present threat of legal action against them by the authorities, and the duty of answering the endless challenges and queries concerning their faith that appeared in print. Meanwhile new converts to the cause had to be welcomed and nurtured, established Friends who were wavering needed to be counselled, practical concerns surrounding money and premises had to be addressed, and, as we shall see, some form of discipline had to be applied to Friends whose words or actions were considered to be inconsistent with core Quaker values. Since the Quakers have always avoided having a single, all-powerful leader, and have never had a written creed or catechism, the questions of who should administer discipline, and what 'core values' needed to be defended, were tricky ones.

London Quaker pioneers like Burrough and Howgill, who had lived in the slower, quieter atmosphere of the countryside and provincial towns, had to contend with these problems in the capital, an unhealthy place, the centre of legal and political power, and home to a bewildering number and variety of people and opinions.

It is hardly surprising, then, that shortly after George Fox and James Nayler arrived in London in 1655, Burrough and Howgill set off for Ireland.

They had reported that London was quiet, but this was hardly Nayler's experience. The Yorkshireman continued the work of the Quaker pioneers in London, speaking to meetings big and small, sometimes several of them in the course of a day, but he soon found that Friends still had many opponents in the capital.

Nayler wrote that 'the devil is so

exceedingly mad that he cries out in open clamours and being confounded is still more mad, and the latter day I saw intents to blood'. During a meeting at a private house, 'hundreds of vain people continued all the while throwing great stones in at the window and broke all the windows, and many stones came in amongst us'. In his *Journal*, George Fox reported that at this time rotten eggs would be thrown into Quaker meetings, and that hostile Londoners would come in making a racket by beating drums and kettles to drown out the preaching of Friends. Fox also mentions that 'wildfire' was thrown into meetings. In the seventeenth century British context, this must refer to some sort of incendiary grenade, like a modern petrol-bomb, of the type that was used by both sides in the civil wars. Since many of the buildings the Quakers would have frequented in London at the time were made of wood, and always had straw scattered about their floors, the use of incendiaries might reflect a serious determination by some Londoners to both kill Quakers and simultaneously burn down the buildings where they met.

Although he was living under constant threat, James Nayler was optimistic enough to write, in a letter to Margaret Fell, 'great is the name of the Lord in this place, His name is become very lovely to some, very terrible to others, mightily doth it spread'.

As we have seen, one way in which Nayler and the early Quakers were able to publicise themselves and their ideas was by participating in public debates. Like the carefully staged debates between Jewish and Christian divines that took place in medieval times, these early modern exchanges could be very interesting, and could attract large, enthusiastic audiences. It may be that their attraction for Londoners in the middle of the seventeenth century was enhanced by the fact that many other forms of entertainment were actively suppressed at the time.

One of the London debates in which Nayler played a prominent part took place at the Glasshouse in Broad Street. This building had been converted into a glass-factory by the Italian glass-maker Jacob Verselini in the previous century. Here, Nayler led the Quaker side in a debate with the Baptists. He met with such success that at least one spectator who had started off on the Baptist side began to lean towards Quakerism. This was Rebecca Travers, the wife of a London tobacconist, who was already in her mid-forties when she attended the debate at the Glasshouse. Later, she wrote that she:

. . . would have been glad to have heard the Baptists get the victory but . . . it proved quite contrary, for the countryman stood up on a form over against the

Baptists and . . . she could feel his words smote them, that one or two of them confessed they were sick and could hold it no longer, and the third . . . shamed himself in bringing scriptures that turned against him, and she was confounded and ashamed that a Quaker should exceed the learned Baptists.

Rebecca, who died, still a committed Quaker, in 1688, at the age of seventy-nine, became convinced after further encounters with Nayler, during one of which he warned her of the dangers of pursuing intellectual knowledge of the type that could erode simple faith. He remarked that such knowledge 'is good to look upon, but not to feed on, for who feeds on knowledge dies to the innocent life'.

London people of all classes were keen to see the new Quaker preacher from the north, including one Lady Darcy, at whose house Nayler spoke. Curious about the Yorkshireman, but shy of being seen and identified at anything resembling a Quaker meeting, many of her ladyship's guests listened to Nayler from behind a screen. It is not clear exactly which Lady Darcy hosted this strange event, but Nayler was able to identify one person who was present: Sir Henry Vane the younger, a prominent politician of the time, whose mother was from an aristocratic family of Essex Darcys. It is possible, then, that Nayler and Vane's hostess on this occasion was a relative of Vane's from his mother's side.

At the time, Sir Henry was equivalent in importance to one of the highest parliamentary generals, but his field of battle and theatre of war was parliament itself. He had very modern, tolerant, democratic views on how the country should be run, and the extent to which minority sects like the Quakers should be left to their own devices, and not harassed by the law. In his *Retired Man's Meditations*, published in 1655, he mentions the Quakers twice, making it clear that he understood the importance of the inward spirit or light to them, but implying that, theologically speaking, they were barking up quite the wrong tree. James Nayler found Vane to be 'drunk with imaginations' and, on the evidence of his *Meditations*, many found Sir Henry's religious ideas whimsical and mysterious.

Henry had clashed with George Fox, who found him 'vain, high, proud, and conceited', at Vane's country seat, Raby Castle, in Anthony Pearson's county, Durham. When Fox visited the castle, he and Vane disagreed over a theological matter not unrelated to those that later surrounded Nayler's second trial for blasphemy. Indeed, Vane's chaplain had practically accused Fox of blasphemy before he even met Sir Henry himself.

When he met the first Quaker, Vane insisted

that he had experienced the inner light Fox preached; but Fox himself implied that he could not have done so, because his ideas about it were wrong. Vane countered by reminding his Quaker visitor that Christ was the Word become flesh; but Fox put more emphasis on the grace of God and the inner light, and less on Christ himself. 'You have climbed up another way than by the door,' said Fox, ' . . . now there is a mountain of earth and imaginations up in you, and from that rises a smoke that has darkened your brain'.

Vane would no doubt have recognised Fox's warning about his climbing up 'another way than by the door': the reference is to John 10: 1, where Jesus says 'He that entereth not by the door into the sheepfold, but climbeth up some other way, the same is a thief and a robber'.

Not surprisingly, Vane soon 'grew into a great fret and a passion, so that there was no room for the truth in his heart'. Later Henry told some friends that if Anthony Pearson and some others had not been with Fox, he would have put George 'out of his house as a mad man'.

As well as satisfying the people of London with his public appearances, Nayler continued to put out printed papers at a terrific rate. It was at this time that Nayler engaged in his pamphlet war with Richard Baxter, the Kidderminster priest.

When he was not speaking and writing, Nayler was attending to the needs of Friends, and soon he was so snowed under with work that he wrote to Burrough and Howgill to return to London to help him.

In his *Retired Man's Meditations*, Sir Henry Vane the Younger compared the Quakers to Moses, who saw the promised land from Mount Pisgah (or Mount Nebo), but could not enter it. Vane wrote that people like the Quakers:

. . . have no abiding city, nor ever enter into the true rest: but only from the top of this Mount Pisgah, they may have a view and prospect into the true land of promise . . .

Vane's comparison is startling, not least because it suggests that the Friends' struggles against persecution in London and elsewhere could be compared to the challenges placed before Moses and the Israelites during their forty years' wandering in the wilderness. The parallel may be more accurate than Vane ever knew, because, like the Israelites, the Quakers of the middle of the seventeenth century were threatened by internal conflicts as well as by attacks from outside their own ranks.

The Old Testament book of Exodus tells us that while Moses was communing with God on Mount Sinai, the Israelites, led by the prophet

Aaron, Moses' brother, raised up a golden calf (called a 'molten calf' in the King James Version). They proceeded to worship the calf, thus reverting to pagan idolatry. Exodus also tells us that the Israelites went naked to worship their idol, a detail that was not lost on the French artist Nicholas Poussin, whose 1633 painting of the adoration of the calf shows Israelites of both genders in various states of undress.

It is tempting to compare the condition of Nayler's followers in London in 1655-6 to the condition of the Israelites who were tempted into pagan idolatry. While George Fox, the Quaker Moses, was often absent from the capital, the discrete group that had formed around James Nayler began to raise up something like an idol, in the shape of James Nayler himself.

As Bernadette Smith points out in her book on Martha Simmonds, the split that affected the Quakers at this time has been compared to the problems of the Early Christian church at Corinth in Greece during the first century AD: problems that are reflected in Paul's first and second letters to the Corinthians, in the New Testament. It is interesting that in his first letter to the Corinthians, Paul reminds them of the error of the Israelites at the time of Moses, many of whom had to perish because they had set up a pagan idol.

The Corinthian Christians, it seems, were splitting up and following different leaders, some saying 'I am of Paul', some 'I of Apollos', others saying they followed one Cephas, and some saying they followed only Christ himself (1 Cor 1: 12).

The situation must have been complicated by the fact that Paul could not often visit Corinth: in this respect the man from Tarsus was like Moses, preoccupied with his conversations with God on Mount Sinai; or George Fox, who could not always be in London to help sort out problems among the Quakers there, sometimes because, like Paul, he was actually in prison somewhere else.

The similarity between the situation among the early Christians in first-century Corinth and the early Quakers in London in 1656 was spotted by Richard Roper, a Lancashire Quaker, who wrote to Margaret Fell that:

It's like there is an evil thing begot amongst Friends in that city, the same as was amongst the church at Corinth, divisions and strife and contention, one saying I am of James, another saying I am of Francis [Howgill] and Edward [Burrough]: and so it's like that Truth will suffer by them.

Roper goes on to imply that in comparison to Quakers further north, the London Friends leave something to be desired:

Truly Friends in the North are rare and precious, very few I find like them, yet this I declare to thee, not to them, lest they should be puffed up.

Paul suggests that where there is such disunity as he discerns among the Corinthians, there must be heresy, and he also mentions concerns about sexual misconduct, including incest. In the same letter, as we have seen, he goes on to assert that the role of women, particularly in church services, should be limited. In 1 Corinthians, this seems to connect with Paul's earlier reflections on the role of women in relation to men, particularly their husbands:

. . . I would have you know, that the head of every man is Christ; and the head of the woman is the man . . . (1 Cor 11, 3)

Similar ideas are to be found in Milton's epic poem *Paradise Lost*, where the author sets out what he perhaps regards as the 'natural' power-relationship between Adam and Eve:

. . . Not equal, as their sex not equal seemed;
For contemplation he and valour formed,
For softness she and sweet attractive grace;
He for God only, she for God in him.

(Book IV, from line 296)

The issue of the role of women in churches, and, by extension, their status in relation to men, is relevant to the crisis in Quakerism at this time because later commentators, looking back on these controversial events, would blame them on some of the London Quaker women, and specifically on Martha Simmonds.

We have already met Martha Simmonds as the sister of George Calvert, and the wife of Thomas Simmonds, who took over much of the role of printer-in-chief to the Quakers from Calvert, his father-in-law. Based in London, where her husband had premises at the Bull and Mouth, Martha could not help but be at the centre of Quaker affairs, and it seems that she was not content to be a mere bystander and observer of those affairs.

Today Martha Simmonds is mainly remembered for her role in the Quaker split of this time, and in the 'fall' of James Nayler from his condition as Quaker leader to the condition of maimed, broken and disgraced convict.

There is, however, more to Martha than her role in the Nayler drama, as recent commentators such as Bernadette Smith have reminded us. In her 2009 book on Simmonds, Smith takes a close look at the small body of Martha's writings that are extant, and even reproduces them in their entirety at the end of her book. These make up a little over a dozen pages, but their content is fascinating and revealing.

Martha Simmonds' tract *When the Lord Jesus Came to Jerusalem* reads like a transcript of a blood-and-thunder sermon given by Martha, perhaps in the style of Nayler's preaching after the Battle of Dunbar, when some found his words more terrifying than the battle itself had been. Here Simmonds attempts to turn the reader's eyes into his own soul where, by the powerful light of God, he will find that he is 'turned out from the presence of God, and art in the gall of bitterness, and the earth is cursed for thy sake'.

Although Simmonds aggressively condemns the reader in her *Jerusalem* tract, she also offers sweet hints of the benefits he will get from repentance, and turning to the divine light:

Now in the still silence, in the light that shines in darkness in thee, thou wilt come to relish that little grain of faith that is held in a pure conscience, and so feel the mountains remove, which presseth down thy soul.

Given that Martha was involved in the Bristol re-enactment of Christ's entry into Jerusalem, it is interesting that one of her tracts should be called *When the Lord Jesus Came to Jerusalem*. In fact, the piece makes little mention of this biblical event, but opens with a reference to Luke 19: 41, where Jesus laments over the future fate of the city of Jerusalem.

In her tract *A Lamentation for the Lost Sheep of the House of Israel* Simmonds again casts shade on her reader, but then narrows down her target to 'the high priests of this nation; and teachers of all sorts of opinions' whom she finds to be greedy, misleading and misled. But again Simmonds offers a beautiful picture of the reward in store for readers who escape from the clutches of these 'idle dumb shepherds'. They will 'come into the fountain that runs forth freely, the streams whereof would refresh your hungry fainting souls'.

In her contributions to *Oh England Thy Time is Come*, a tract which was probably written the year after the Bristol incident, Simmonds reveals an intense, personal and mystical side to her faith. Here a perfect figure, a precious 'Vessel' who may be both Jesus and James Nayler rolled into one, is the author's 'beloved', whom she will follow 'unto death'. It is implied that this figure is the fulfilment of the spiritual longing that had caused her to seek in vain for enlightenment for no less that fourteen years: this desperate quest is described in her *Lamentation*.

Like many of the Quaker writers of her time, Simmonds is so familiar with the language and imagery of the Bible that it is sometimes hard to spot when the biblical takes over from the personal, and vice-versa. In *Oh England*, her longing for the 'Vessel' is stated in terms reminiscent of the sensuality of the Old Testament Song of Songs.

With their rich mix of feeling and imagery, their hints at vast emotional and spiritual forces, and their sense of the immanence of the biblical world, Martha Simmonds' few surviving writings seem to defy the accusations of insincerity that earlier commentators, including George Whitehead, made against her. Indeed her writings are so sincere and intense that they seem to preclude the possibility that Simmonds attempted to abuse her role in the early Quaker movement in London merely to gain power and status by manipulating James Nayler. Simmonds' writings suggest that her sense that she was living in a time of unique and immediate spiritual significance made her impatient with the ways of some of her fellow Quaker preachers, and determined to make the whole Quaker movement more urgent, assertive, fearless and confrontational.

In an attempt, perhaps, to belittle Martha Simmonds' importance, George Whitehead wrote in his *Impartial Account* of Nayler's life that 'a few forward, conceited, imaginary women, especially Martha Simmonds and some others, under pretence of some divine motions, grew somewhat turbulent'. (Whitehead's *Impartial Account* appears at the beginning of his *Collection of Sundry Books . . . by James Nayler*, published in 1716. This short biography of Nayler is called an *Impartial Account* in its chapter heading, but an *Impartial Relation* on the whole book's title-page.)

Unfortunately, the quotation from Whitehead's *Account* printed at the start of the paragraph above includes several words that have changed their meanings in modern English. By 'conceited' we now tend to mean something like 'excessively proud', but in seventeenth century English a 'conceited' person was one whose head was full of ideas or 'conceits' - today we might say 'conceptions'. Whitehead's context implies that he felt that the conceits in the heads of Martha and her associates were harmful ones. Likewise, George's application of the word 'imaginary' to the women does not suggest that he thought of them as fictitious, but rather full of imaginings. The 'divine motions' Whitehead implies that the women were pretending to, or simulating in some way, are the instructions of the Holy Spirit.

In an article published in the *Journal of the Friends Historical Society* in 1972, A.W. Brink asserted that in 'tempting' Nayler to split from the main body of the London Quakers Martha Simmonds was acting like Eve, or even like

Satan himself, as depicted in Milton's *Paradise Lost*. In this, Brink was echoing Whitehead's attitude: George blamed the 'many ways, wiles and devices' of 'Satan, the old Adversary' before going on to name 'Martha Simmonds and some others' as the leading human actors in the drama that was then unfolding.

X. Signs

Although what Nayler, Fox, Simmonds and their associates did to spread the word before 1656 could disrupt public order and, in particular, disturb the lives and work of 'steeple-house' ministers, their approach was fairly conventional and respectable in comparison to the activities of some others who went by the name of Quakers at the time.

Richard Sale, the man who was repeatedly stuffed into 'Little Ease' in Chester's Northgate Prison, had attracted the attention of the authorities by acting out his beliefs and his message in a way that reminds us of James Nayler's controversial entry into Bristol in 1656.

In 1654, Sale went through the streets of Chester bare-footed and bare-legged, dressed in sackcloth, with ashes on his head, holding sweet flowers in his right hand and stinking weeds in his left. Going in sackcloth and ashes is an ancient symbol of mourning and repentance that is often met with in the Bible. The people of Chester were astonished to see Sale in this condition, though some of them were able to recover from their astonishment long enough to set their dogs on him. We know that three years later, after the trial of James Nayler, Sale also walked around in Chester in broad daylight with a lighted candle, to show how candles should not be used in church services.

Like Richard Sale, George Fox himself had been moved to abandon his footwear to complete a 'sign' he was inspired to enact. In the winter of 1651 Fox had seen the three spires of Lichfield Cathedral from a distance. The sight of these had 'struck at his life', and he set off as the crow flies, over hedges and ditches, to get to the city as quickly as possible.

When he got about a mile away, Fox left his shoes with some shepherds and proceeded to stomp up and down the streets of Lichfield in his stockinged feet crying out 'Woe unto the bloody city of Lichfield'. It was market-day, a busy time, but nobody laid hands on Fox, who thought he saw blood running down the streets. Later, he discovered a dubious legend about a massacre of Christians that had happened in the city in Roman times. This, it seems, had inspired his 'sign'.

The Lichfield incident, which is now commemorated by a plaque in the city, is sometimes used out of context by people writing short histories of the early Quakers, or of the sects of seventeenth-century Britain in general. It thus comes to represent 'the crazy stuff those people did'; but in the context of George Fox's life, Lichfield is really the exception that proves the rule. Roaming the streets without shoes and bellowing at the top of his voice was precisely the type of thing Fox did not usually do.

Unlike Sale, Fox had not abandoned his stockings and gone bare-legged into Lichfield, but other early Quakers went much further in casting off clothing as part of a 'sign'. In 1654 Elizabeth Fletcher, a seventeen-year old Quaker girl from Kendal,

went naked through the streets of [Oxford], as a sign against that hypocritical profession they then made there, being then Presbyterians and Independents, which profession she told them the Lord would strip them of

Whether Oxford's all-male student body was able to take in Elizabeth's message about Presbyterianism and Independency while she exhibited her nudity to them is unclear. It seems likely that the sight of Elizabeth undraped suggested things other than theology to at least some of them.

That Quakers like Elizabeth Fletcher felt

moved to use signs such as nudity to put across their message reflects the determination of early Friends to fight on all fronts, and to use what we might term a variety of media to bring the truth to the unconvinced. One problem with more visual forms of communication, such as going naked, or re-enacting key events from the gospels, is that the symbolism employed can easily be misinterpreted. Nudity in particular is a very ambiguous symbol. In the twenty-first century, it tends to be associated with sex, yet in the iconography of classic western paintings and sculpture from the medieval period right up to Nayler's time, nude or scantily-clad figures can represent purity, beauty, freedom, innocence; even poverty, vulnerability, humiliation and distress, as well as sexuality.

The 'problem' with many works of art that use male or female nudes is that while the naked figure may be there to represent, for example, the element of Water (as in a painting by James Nayler's contemporary Peter Paul Rubens) the figure may be realistic enough to become, in the eyes of some beholders, a sexually provocative element in the work of art.

The use of nudity as a protest is represented in the English tradition by the medieval story of Lady Godiva, who is said to have ridden through the city of Coventry, without the benefit of clothing, to alert her husband, Earl Leofric, to the fact that his excessive taxation was impoverishing the people.

The story of Peeping Tom is always associated with that of Lady Godiva. While everybody else in Coventry respectfully averted their eyes from the naked rider, Tom looked through a key-hole and was instantly struck blind. He had misinterpreted the lady's ride: he thought it was an opportunity to leer at a naked woman; but such visual signs are easier to misinterpret than written statements, or spoken testimony, during which listeners may have the opportunity to ask questions and thus pin down the exact meaning the speaker is trying to convey.

In the cut-and-thrust of the pamphlet warfare in which Nayler and others engaged, there was also the opportunity to interact with an author and ask for clarification of his or her ideas; but the oppositional nature of this interaction tended to mean that the long lists of queries exchanged by authors were more like grenades thrown through windows than cloths used to clean them and promote clarity. Although the opportunity for a fruitful exchange of ideas was thus lost because of prejudice and suspicion, it is hard to see how such an exchange could be conducted around a visual 'sign' such as Elizabeth Fletcher walking naked through Oxford, or Nayler and co. riding into Bristol. Because of the nature of such 'signs', any discussion of them tended to be conducted as part of a subsequent trial, or in discussions between concerned Quakers about whether or not such a sign should have been enacted in the first place.

It is hardly surprising that William Shakespeare, the ultimate word-smith, should have suggested, in some lines spoken by Hamlet, that though purely visual forms of communication may appeal to uneducated people, they may be impossible to interpret. The prince tells us that the 'groundlings', who paid a penny to watch a play standing up, were 'capable of nothing but *inexplicable* dumb-shows and noise' (my italics; *Hamlet*, Act 3, sc. 2).

Elizabeth Fletcher worked closely with another Elizabeth, surnamed Leavens, who was also a native of Kendal. Both were very harshly treated at Oxford, where they were whipped. Elizabeth Leavens later married Thomas Holme, also a Kendal Quaker, who was imprisoned at Chester, in 1655, for going through the streets naked as a sign. During his time at the Chester jail in the previous year, Holme had slept on the floor (because he believed he should not sleep on the bed provided) sang loudly at all hours, and saw visions of a light 'so glorious it dazzled my eyes'.

The Quaker fondness for outré gestures did

not entirely disappear after the severe check the movement suffered subsequent to the trial of James Nayler; although many writers note a general calming-down among Quakers following that time. The London musician Solomon Eccles may not have become a Quaker until as late as 1659, when he became convinced that he should give up music altogether. He attempted to burn all his instruments on Tower Hill, but passers-by stopped him, so that he was forced to stamp on them instead of incinerating them. In the 1660s, Eccles was often seen walking around London naked, with a bowl of fire and brimstone balanced on his head, crying out, 'Repent! Repent!' In 1668, the diarist Samuel Pepys saw Eccles in this condition, but smeared all over with excrement.

Despite his extreme behaviour, Solomon Eccles seems to have remained on good terms with the leading Quakers of his time, though occasionally there were tensions. He even accompanied George Fox and others on an important trip to the West Indies in 1671. Given his tendency to discard his clothes before leaving home, it seems ironic that, after he gave up music, Eccles had become a tailor.

Although an attempt to enter the English city of Bristol in a way that mirrored Christ's entry into Jerusalem on Palm Sunday would probably not lead to an arrest today, people who go naked as a sign, or as part of a protest, or out of sheer eccentricity, can expect to be arrested in twenty-first century Britain, unless they restrict themselves to nudist camps and beaches. The fact that Nayler's Bristol 'sign', which lacked any element of nudity, met with a far harsher punishment than the authorities were then willing to hand out to people who went naked shows how much British society has changed.

True, some of Nayler's followers took off their cloaks to cast them before James's horse, which was unfortunate given the rainy weather, but presumably these garments were recovered as the party processed into Bristol through the Ratcliffe Gate.

Martha Simmonds, who was perhaps nearly as central to the Bristol incident as James Nayler himself, was no stranger to outré gestures, visual or otherwise, enacted to promote the gospel. As we have seen, she would walk about the streets of cities and towns 'crying repentance'; and she had resorted to the ancient signs of both nakedness and sackcloth and ashes to draw attention to her message. What distinguished Simmonds and her group from other Quaker activists of the time, however, was their willingness to disrupt meetings led by fellow-Quakers with whom they disagreed.

According to George Whitehead's *Impartial Account* of Nayler's life, Martha Simmonds and her band of 'forward, conceited, imaginary women' began interrupting public meetings in London led by Edward Burrough and Francis Howgill.

We have already met Edward Burrough: rather less is known about Howgill, born at Todthorne near Grayrigg in Westmorland around 1618, although he seems to have come from a similar yeoman background to that of James Nayler. Like Nayler, Howgill may have been a farmer at one time – he may also have gained some income from working as a tailor, like the eccentric London Quaker Solomon Eccles. What makes Francis different from many of the Quakers of his generation is that he seems to have been university-educated, and after flirtations with the Independents and the Baptists, he established himself as a Church of England minister at Colton in Cumbria.

When he encountered George Fox at a place called Firbank Fell, also in Cumbria, in 1652, he was so taken aback that, as he later told Fox, anyone 'might have killed him with a crab-apple'. By this time, he had already defended Fox as a preacher at nearby Sedbergh, saying that George spoke 'with authority, and not as the scribes'; an attribute of Jesus himself. Later, Howgill experienced a gradual process of convincement, and became a Quaker.

In January 1653, Howgill also showed solidarity with James Nayler by speaking in his defence before the justices at Appleby. Refusing, in true Quaker fashion, to remove his hat out of respect for the magistrates, it was thrown into the fire, and he himself was thrown into prison for five months.

Howgill's encounters with Fox in Cumbria in 1652 place him at the time and place of what many regard as the real beginning of the Quaker movement. True, by this time Fox had been an itinerant preacher for some years, but it was in this area of the north-west of England during the Quaker *annus mirabilis* of 1652 that a group called the Westmorland Seekers, and others such as Howgill and Margaret Fell, took Fox's message so seriously that the Quaker movement began to grow rapidly, and in earnest.

Martha Simmonds and her group could hardly question the Quaker *bona fides* of Howgill and Burrough, but they nevertheless disrupted their public meetings and, in the words of George Whitehead, showed 'indiscretion' and did 'hurt . . . in some meetings'.

There is an account of a London meeting disrupted by Simmonds in a letter written by the Lancashire Quaker Richard Hubberthorne to Margaret Fell. According to Hubberthorne, Simmonds broke the silence of the meeting with a long speech accusing the Quakers present of failing to support her, and not bearing the cross, as Quakers should. It seems that she went on to try to persuade those present to follow her, and forsake meetings such as the one where all this happened. 'Then she fell on singing with an unclean spirit, and the substance of that which she said in her singing was "innocency, innocency," many times over, for the space of an hour or more'.

Hubberthorne tried to interrupt her and 'bring that under the fear and dread of God which she would have raised into lightness', but Simmonds continued singing, then changed the words of her song, accusing those present of being the Beast of the book of Revelation, and identifying Hubberthorne himself as the head of the Beast.

Hubberthorne was not the only one who tried to discourage Martha's disruptive behaviour. According to Whitehead, Edward Burrough and Francis Howgill reproved Martha 'and her party', 'manifesting their dislike thereto, seeing their forwardness', and in response Martha and the others complained to James Nayler, 'endeavouring to set him against them, and to draw a judgement from him against them'.

Nayler 'was afraid to pass judgement upon his brethren as they desired', and in response

Martha 'fell into a passion in a kind of mourning, or weeping, and bitterly crying out with a mournful shrill voice'.

According to Whitehead, who claims that he had discussed all this with Nayler himself in Westmorland in 1657, the effect of Martha's 'mourning, or weeping' was to make the Yorkshireman sad, sorrowful, dejected and disconsolate. Eventually 'he came to be clouded in his understanding, bewildered, and at a loss in his judgement'.

Whitehead implies that while he was in this weakened condition Nayler was unable to put a stop to the continued outlandish behaviour of 'those persons who had complained and cried to him for judgement against his brethren', who now 'cried him up publicly in divers places, bowing and kneeling before him, magnifying him with high appellations'. This, says Whitehead, made 'a fool and gazing-stock' of Nayler.

Although Whitehead knew Nayler well, and called his biography of his friend an 'impartial account', the author certainly had an agenda when he wrote his version of events: an agenda which evidently included a determination to cast shade on Simmonds and her followers, and to try to polish up the tarnished reputation of James Nayler.

Whitehead's attempt to suggest that Nayler

was somehow hypnotised or stupefied by Simmonds, and robbed of any ability to make rational decisions, almost suggests that Simmonds was some kind of evil fairy or witch, able to enchant the Yorkshireman: indeed the Quaker William Dewsbury and others, both Quakers and non-Quakers, suggested that some sort of black art might have had a role to play. Dewsbury, a Yorkshireman like Nayler, wrote in an angry letter to Martha Simmonds that 'the righteous seed is burdened with thee, who hath in thy deceitful practice opened the mouth of the enemies of God to blaspheme his name, & *through thy sorcery* hath abused the simplicity' (my italics).

It seems unlikely, however, that Martha's influence alone could have led to Nayler's torpor at this time, which is well attested in other sources. Bittle for one speculates that a combination of the stresses bearing down on James, as well as Simmonds' influence, caused him to go very quiet. Whitehead's tendency to put the blame on Martha and some other women also ignores the fact that several men were involved, including Martha's own husband.

Whitehead's application of words like 'forward' to Simmonds and her followers is bound to raise the hackles of readers who have any modern sense of the equality of the sexes. The word calls to mind old-fashioned English injunctions such as 'know your place', which seem to be particularly offensive when applied to women.

The source of the version of events that Whitehead gives in his *Impartial Account* can also be questioned. He claims that he heard it from Nayler himself at Great Strickland in Westmorland in 1657, the year after the Bristol incident; but Nayler would have been locked up in Bridewell prison in London at that time. It is likely that Whitehead, who was writing in 1716, over half a century after Nayler's death, when he himself was in his eighties, had become confused about dates and places.

From Whitehead, we get the impression that Simmonds had no real reason to disrupt Quaker meetings or attempt to drive a wedge between certain groups within the Quaker leadership. This can hardly have been the case, but in fact it is difficult, over three hundred years later, to discern exactly what it was about some of the leading Quakers of the time that offended Martha. In his book on Nayler, William Bittle admits that Simmonds' motivation still remains unclear.

Nayler's condition at this time, which many Friends attributed to the influence of Simmonds and her circle, caused some who were not from the Simmonds group to try to separate the Yorkshireman from Martha and others, who were regarded as bad influences.

Concerned Friends spirited Nayler away to Bristol, but this 'intervention', as we might call it today, was not entirely successful. Simmonds and some companions soon arrived at what was then England's second biggest city, but when they came into a meeting to be with Nayler he was taken off to 'a house by the orchard'. Simmonds followed, and later she claimed that Quakers, including Burrough and Howgill 'plucked me and the rest exceedingly & used us very sorely, in so much that J. Nayler did sweat exceedingly, and we were in danger of our lives; & they threw me down the stairs'.

Simmonds' account, quoted above, is from a 1656 anti-Quaker pamphlet called *Satan Enthoned in His Chair of Pestilence*, written by a hostile Bristol priest called Ralph Farmer, of whom more later.

The idea that the Quakers had pushed Martha down some stairs was contradicted by the Bristol Quaker George Bishop, who was there at the time. In his 1657 pamphlet *The Throne of Truth Exalted Over the Powers Of Darkness* he claimed that Simmonds could not have been pushed down any stairs, as there were no stairs in the building in question.

The orchard mentioned by Farmer, where Martha Simmonds is supposed to have been pushed downstairs, was the orchard of the old

Dominican friary in Bristol, which then belonged to Dennis Hollister. Hollister was a wealthy Bristol grocer and land-owner who had been converted to Quakerism in London.

We get a snap-shot of the tension Hollister's conversion led to among his acquaintances from *The Quaker's Jesus*, a pamphlet published by Hollister's fellow Bristolian William Grigge in 1658. It seems that Hollister had lent Grigge a book by Nayler, almost certainly *An Answer to the Book Called The Perfect Pharisee*, published in 1654. As its title suggests, Nayler's pamphlet was an attempt to refute the accusations contained in a slightly earlier pamphlet, by Thomas Weld, a priest of the Independent persuasion who relished religious controversy.

Grigge seems to have had his own copy of Weld's pamphlet, but he returned his borrowed copy of Nayler's *Answer* to Hollister at his shop in the high street.

'Now you have read some truths after your lies, set forth by the priests,' said Hollister on this occasion. Grigge replied to the effect that Weld had written the truth, but Nayler's *Answer* was 'a pack of lies'. Hollister answered that some people would believe nothing but lies, but, as he left, Grigge remarked that there was a generation of men that made lies their refuge, and they were the Quakers.

In his *Quaker's Jesus* Grigge states that he hopes, 'for old acquaintance sake' 'that this man D. H. may have repentance given him, and turn again to his old puritanical principles, from whence he is deeply fallen, that he may not go on to this blasphemer's height,' meaning that Grigge hoped that Hollister would not become a 'blasphemer' like Nayler.

Grigge maintained his faith in the truth of Weld's *Perfect Pharisee*, and used it as a source for much of the material in his *Quaker's Jesus*.

Before Hollister had converted to Quakerism, he had been a Baptist elder, and a founding member of a Baptist church which was the first non-conformist church to be set up in Bristol. If the 'house by the orchard' was the old Dominican friary, which Hollister owned, then it certainly had and has stairs. Now known as Blackfriars or Quakers Friars, the surviving buildings are two-storey structures.

During this stay in Bristol, the Nayler group slept at the White Hart in Broadstreet, of which Hollister was joint landlord.

XI. Launceston and Exeter

Since the Quakers of the time were widely scattered throughout the British Isles and beyond, it is hardly surprising that some Friends' attempts to intervene in the alarming Nayler/Simmonds situation should have taken the form of letters. Luckily a number of these, including some from George Fox, and William Dewsbury's letter to Simmonds accusing her of 'sorcery', have survived.

The reason why George Fox could not intervene personally in this time of crisis was because he was in prison at Launceston in Cornwall. There really was no good reason to imprison him and his companions there, but this was the time of the rule of the major-generals, some of whom gave themselves a great deal of latitude about whom they punished and why.

The Friends at Launceston had to wait in prison for nine weeks until the assizes were held, when they were accused of, among other things, distributing troublesome papers, travelling without a pass and refusing the oath of abjuration.

The oath of abjuration was the Interregnum equivalent of the old oath of allegiance, which the Quakers would not swear to because they refused to swear at all, following Christ's injunction in the Gospel of Matthew:

Swear not at all; neither by heaven; for it is God's throne: Nor by the earth; for it is his footstool: neither by Jerusalem; for it is the city of the great King. Neither shalt thou swear by thy head, because thou canst not make one hair white or black. But let your communication be, Yea, yea; Nay, nay: for whatsoever is more than these cometh of evil.

(Matthew 5, 33-37)

In those days, the conditions Quakers endured in prison were likely to depend on how much they were prepared to pay to the jailer. At Launceston, Fox and his company had been paying seven shillings a week for themselves, and the same for their horses; and conditions had not been too bad. When they stopped their payments, they were cast into a room called Doomsdale, unimaginably filthy, about which it was said that few who stayed there ever came out alive. When an official complaint was made, the Friends were allowed to clean out Doomsdale themselves, and were even permitted to buy their food in the local town, and walk in the Castle Green.

Fox's jailers would not, however, permit him to travel to Bristol to see James Nayler, and James and his group decided to visit Fox at Launceston.

They set off from Bristol on the morning of the first of August, 1656, a group of five. Of these, Francis Howgill and John Audland only went part of the way, peeling off after about fifteen miles. Writing to Edward Burrough, Howgill related how Nayler 'did one while weep exceedingly' as they travelled, and implied that, by a miracle, Martha Simmonds and her group had been scattered: indeed, Howgill admitted that he had no idea where Martha was. 'A mighty thing was in it that they should be so parted – even by nothing, as to the outward'.

Soon the remaining three travellers were arrested under one of the laws that George Fox was supposed to have infringed: travelling without a pass. The authorities seemed untroubled by the fact that they actually had a pass signed by John Desborough, who had been a parliamentary general in the civil wars, was major-general for the south-west, and also happened to be Oliver Cromwell's brother-in-law.

On the eleventh of August, Henry Fell, Margaret Fell's son and an active Quaker, wrote to her from Bristol that 'there was no passing that way, for there is watches all the country over that no Friends can pass to Launceston . . . but are taken up & had to prison'.

Nayler and his two companions, Nicholas Ganniclliffe and John Bolton, had been arrested by the mayor of Okehampton in Devon, and before they were locked up in jail at Exeter one Judge Steele fined them, for not removing their hats. Henry Fell reported to his mother that there were seven other Quakers prisoners at Exeter: John Audland told her that there were twenty-three in total.

Imprisoned at Exeter, Nayler promptly began an intense and prolonged fast, something which had become a regular habit with him. Thomas Rawlinson, a Lancashire Quaker and fellow-prisoner, wrote to Margaret Fell that:

. . . he ate no bread but one little bit, for a whole month, & there was about a fortnight when I came to him he took no manner of food, but some days a pint of white wine, & some days a gill mingled with water; but now he eats meat.

It may surprise modern readers that Nayler was able to take 'a pint of white wine' on an empty stomach, but in those days wine in general was much weaker than it is today.

His diet, his imprisonment and the

controversy surrounding him no doubt combined to make James continue very quiet and apparently depressed at this time; but when John Stubbs, a Quaker missionary who was probably from Durham, visited him in early September, he was able to write to Margaret Fell that both Nayler and Thomas Rawlinson were well, though they slept on straw with the 'pirates'. As to Nayler's mental condition, Stubbs said that he was now 'pretty', by which Fell's correspondent meant not that he was good-looking, but that he was generally in a good condition. Switching to metaphor, Stubbs added that 'the rotten rags and dust which he was covered with is near taken off'.

The numerous visits the Quakers in prison had at this time, the way that they were often able to leave their confinement to meet visiting Friends outside, and the fact that they were often able to send and receive letters in an unrestricted way, reflects the rather *ad hoc* organisation of the seventeenth-century justice system. That their jailers were often happy to let their Quaker prisoners go wandering around the local town may also be a function of the fact that many Friends were practically in prison by choice, because they refused to pay a sometimes modest fine or fee, or swear a simple oath, that would have led to their release. Since they were in effect prisoners of their own consciences, and often explicitly welcomed the testing time of suffering that imprisonment represented, they were unlikely, so their jailers no doubt reasoned, to attempt to escape.

Some of these freedoms may have been won by the simple expedient of paying a small fee to the jailer: the Friends locked up at Exeter in 1656 paid to be allowed to hold Quaker meetings for worship, and we have already learned that, for a while, Fox paid seven shillings a week (the equivalent of perhaps thirty pounds today) for improved conditions at Launceston.

As at Launceston, banged-up Quakers could sometimes escape very poor and restrictive prison conditions by complaining to higher authorities, and the masters of some prisons would have known that some people in high places were sympathetic to the Quakers' cause. It seems that at Derby, where Fox spent a year locked up from 1650 to 1651, the 'keeper' of the prison, who was at first scornful of the Quakers, was eventually so impressed by George Fox's evident sanctity that he told him 'I have been as a lion against you; but now I come like a lamb, and like the jailer that came to Paul and Silas trembling,' referring to an incident involving St Paul and his companion Silas recorded in Acts 16: 29.

We learn in Fox's *Journal* that this prison 'keeper' (as Fox calls him, echoing the word used in the King James version of Acts) actually wanted George to escape, because he had become weighed down with guilt about his imprisonment. The keeper told his wife:

I have seen the day of judgement, and I saw George there; and I was afraid of him, because I had done him so much wrong, and spoken so much against him to the ministers and professors, and to the justices, and in taverns and alehouses.

The solution he came up with was to persuade the local justices to allow Fox to 'walk a mile'. George told them that if they showed him how long a mile was, he would be happy to do so, but he made it clear that he would not run away, because he 'was not of that spirit'. Later the jailer admitted that the 'walk a mile' scheme had indeed been devised to allow Fox to go on the lam.

A fortnight or so after John Stubbs's visit to Exeter, the Lancashire Quaker Richard Hubberthorne was dismayed to find that Martha Simmonds was with Nayler there, and, in Hubberthorne's words to Margaret Fell, 'he was too much subject to her'. Richard had, of course, clashed with Martha at least once before, when she had disrupted one of his Quaker meetings by singing 'innocency, innocency' over and over, and calling him the head of the Beast.

Like Nayler, Hubberthorne was a veteran of the civil wars, but as a Quaker he was a gentle, peace-loving man who wrote to Margaret Fell that in Exeter prison 'dear & tender love from my soul flowed forth to him' [Nayler]. The soul-contact thus described caused James to open his heart to Hubberthorne, and he 'let forth himself to me', but the meetings of the two men were always interrupted by Martha Simmonds, who would call Nayler away and break the spell.

Before she reached Nayler at Exeter, Simmonds had visited George Fox at Launceston with her associate Hannah Stranger, the wife of a London comb-maker. There, according to Hubberthorne, Simmonds had 'exalted herself & judged him as she had judged me & worse; & said he might come down out of his wisdom & subtlety, & much of that nature'. Fox related that Martha 'came singing in my face', and that she told him that his heart was rotten.

Fox was released from Launceston Castle on September the ninth, but delayed visiting Nayler and his group at Exeter until the twentieth.

There then followed a series of meetings between the two men, in the prison itself, in a nearby inn, and even in the street. Viewed as a whole, these encounters resembled a summit meeting between two world leaders where, despite the efforts of the anxious diplomats scurrying around, the leaders do not hit it off: personalities get in the way of the issues, the issues prevent any personal bonding, there are misunderstandings and *faux pas*, a great opportunity is wasted, and peace and understanding prove elusive.

The scurrying diplomats at Exeter included Richard Hubberthorne who, although he evidently wanted peace between the two men, was quite certain in his own mind that Nayler had to cast off 'those filthy spirits that was about him,' meaning Martha Simmonds and her group. Presumably, these 'filthy spirits' were what Stubbs had referred to as 'rotten rags and dust'.

At a meeting for worship in the prison, Nayler, and perhaps some others, left before the meeting was concluded, because Fox had 'judged' them. The next day, after a surprisingly amicable meeting between Fox and Nayler at the inn, George came and called for James at the prison, but he would not come.

Later in the week, Fox came to visit Nayler in the prison again, where he criticised the Yorkshireman for, among other things, some words he had spoken to him in the street the day before, when he had urged Fox to 'take heed of lying and false accusing'.

Fox's words caused Nayler to weep, and he offered Fox an apple, which he refused. Nayler asked if he could kiss Fox's hand, but when Fox offered it, Nayler would not. Then Fox said 'it is my foot,' seemingly intending that James should kiss his foot, which would have been a sign of obedience to the first Quaker. This Nayler also refused to do.

This particular encounter at Exeter is seen as a key episode in Nayler's story, and indeed it is described in considerable detail by Richard Hubberthorne in a letter to Margaret Fell. Hubberthorne told Fell that this strange conversation, with its awkward, incomplete physical gestures, happened while Fox was standing on a higher part of the floor than the place where Nayler and others were standing. Fox tried to draw Nayler out of that place, but he would not come. At first, Fox refused to offer his hand to Nayler because, in his elevated position, he would have had to bow down to do so. The fact that there were witnesses, including Hubberthorne himself, must have made both James and George wary of putting a foot or a word wrong.

No doubt the wariness of both Fox and Nayler at this time was enhanced by what had passed between them before James had been arrested: Fox's spoken and written admonishments were no doubt in Nayler's mind, and Fox's recent confrontation with

Martha Simmonds and Hannah Stranger was doubtless in his.

In his account of his visit to Exeter in his *Journal*, Fox does not mention the 'foot' episode, which, if it was an attempt to make Nayler perform a public act of abasement to him, is not an easy thing for a modern reader to accept:

The next day I spoke to James Nayler again; and he slighted what I said, was dark, and much out; yet he would have come and kissed me. But I said that since he had turned against the power of God, I could not receive his show of kindness. The Lord moved me to slight him, and to set the power of God over him. So after I had been warring with the world, there was now a wicked spirit risen amongst Friends to war against. I admonished him and his company.

James Nayler's eventual release from Exeter prison came about as a result of a curious train of events.

Soon after James and his companions were imprisoned in August, a Quaker woman turned up at the house of the aforementioned General John Desborough, major-general of the south-west of England. The woman claimed that God had instructed her to present herself in this way, and she was soon working as a nurse to Desborough's wife Jane, who was gravely ill.

The Quaker did not effect a cure through her nursing of the sister of Oliver Cromwell – the lady died that year – but she did manage to win the trust of the family, and was able to convince the general that Nayler and his group should be released. The volunteer Quaker nurse was none other than Martha Simmonds.

This episode shows yet another side of Simmonds' complex character. The intense, emotional and mystical writer could also be a rowdy, disruptive presence in public meetings and, paradoxically, a careful, trustworthy nurse able to inspire immediate and lasting confidence and gratitude in a distraught family.

Like so much in this story, Simmonds' interaction with the Desboroughs is open to interpretation. In his *Satan Enthroned in his Chair of Pestilence*, the anti-Quaker writer Ralph Farmer characterises Simmonds as a 'notable piece' and a 'serpent' whom the Desboroughs had incautiously let into their house, thus aiding her scheme for 'the enlargement of these wretched blasphemers', meaning the Quaker prisoners at Exeter.

As well as hostile accounts like Farmer's pamphlet, the sources for Nayler's Exeter imprisonment include letters exchanged between various concerned parties, including a significant number addressed to Margaret Fell at Swarthmore Hall. Although he was to some extent coming out of his shell as far as speech was concerned, Nayler was writing little at this time, and we do not have his written point of view from this part of 1656.

Nayler evidently wrote a letter to Margaret Fell containing some of his views around this time, but this letter has been lost, and all we have is Fell's reply. That remarkable letter is dated the fifteenth of October 1656, i.e. just days before the notorious Bristol incident.

Fell's letter is deeply spiritual and highly emotional, and like many other letters addressed to Nayler at this time it implores him to modify his mind and his behaviour. Fell suggests that her correspondent should do this by embracing a larger measure of humility. Referring to Nayler's lost letter, Margaret remarks that 'I could receive and bear what thou had written in it if thou had kept in subjection, love and unity as thou did express in thy letter'. Later in the letter, Fell implies that Nayler should be more like the Lamb of God:

I am sure the Lamb in his suffering is in subjection, not resisting nor exalting; but in the time of his suffering he is servant to all the seed.

To judge from her letter, it would seem that Margaret had a sense that the central error that James was committing was his suspicion of, and rebellion against, George Fox. The nearest thing we have to a quotation from the lost letter is where Margaret remarks 'thou saith George is burying thy name that he may raise his own'. This suggests that at least one aspect of the painful rift in the Quaker ranks at this time was indeed a power struggle between the two men.

A startling characteristic of Fell's October 1656 letter to Nayler is that she uses extravagant terms for George Fox, perhaps in an attempt to persuade Nayler to find humility by revering him as much as she herself evidently did. To her, Fox is 'him to whom all nations shall bow,' a name 'to which every knee must bow', 'the promise of the Father to the seed', 'thy father and thy life' and even 'thy first husband'.

After his encounters with Fox at Exeter, during which both men sometimes exhibited an almost childish unwillingness to be reconciled, Nayler may not have been ready to think of Fox in the same way that he had thought of him in 1652, when he addressed him in a letter as 'My father, my father, the glory of Israel'.

In her despair at the rift between Nayler and her future husband, which she said grieved her spirit, Fell declared in her letter that 'I could lie down at thy feet that thou might trample upon me, for thy good'.

Unfortunately it is very unlikely that Nayler ever saw Margaret's letter: whether or not the reading of it would have changed the course of his life can never be known. It may have been returned unread to Swarthmore, Nayler having moved on to do things that would grieve Margaret Fell's heart even more. It seems that when Nayler made his fateful entry into Bristol in October 1656, the letter was in the possession of the aforementioned George Bishop, a Bristol Quaker who witnessed much of what went on in the city at that time, but was certainly not in agreement with Nayler's actions.

XII. Ratcliffe Rubicon

The city of Bristol, the scene of the event that will forever be linked to Nayler's name, had not had a peaceful introduction to Quakerism.

The diarist John Evelyn visited the city at the end of July 1654, just weeks before the Quakers John Camm and John Audland first arrived in Bristol as missionaries in early September of the same year. Evelyn wrote that Bristol was:

a city emulating London, not for its large extent, but manner of building, shops, bridge, traffic, exchange, market-place, etc. . . . The city wholly mercantile, as standing near the famous Severn, commodiously for Ireland, and the Western world. Here I first saw the manner of refining sugar and casting it into loaves, where we had a collection of eggs fried in the sugar furnace, together with excellent Spanish wine.

Evelyn had an eye for important details, and his mention of Bristol's commercial links with Ireland and 'the Western world', and of sugar and Spanish wine, reminds us that the city, that lies on the river Avon, a few miles inland from the Severn, was ideally placed to trade with Wales, Ireland, western Europe and the Americas.

During the civil wars, the city had started off as a parliamentary stronghold, but was then captured in July 1643 by a royalist force commanded by Prince Rupert of the Rhine, nephew of Charles I.

In his 2009 book *Bristol in the Civil War,* John Lynch tells us that Bristol's factories, and its easy access to the sea, made it easier for the royalists to stay in the war, while they held it. A great deal of gunpowder was manufactured in the city, for instance, and weapons could be imported into Bristol from mainland Europe.

The city was regained by Thomas Fairfax for the parliamentary side in 1645, although Prince Rupert was present to defend it. This constituted a major disgrace for Rupert, who was banished in 1646. The loss of Bristol was also a serious blow to the royalist cause.

By 1654, when the Quakers set out to convince as many Bristolians as they could of the rightness of their message, the city had more or less recovered from the civil wars, which had ended in 1651. War-damaged structures had undergone repairs, shipbuilding and the manufacture of gunpowder were both back on their feet, and wine was being imported, though on a smaller scale than it had been before the conflict. Among other important commodities, tallow, and preserved meat and fish, were being imported from Ireland, and imports of tobacco, and the sugar Evelyn had seen being made into the large, bullet-shaped 'loaves', were increasing.

In 1655, the Bristol Presbyterian minister Ralph Farmer wrote in his pamphlet *The Great Mysteries of Godliness and Ungodliness* that:

A while ago there came to this city of Bristol, certain morris-dancers from the north, by two and two, two and two, with an intent here to exercise some spiritual cheats; or (as may well be suspected) to carry on some levelling design. And our soldiers here, having nothing else to do (unless work of their own making, that they might seem to be necessary) struck in with them in their quaking. And myself, with some other of my brethren in the ministry here, being (by the magistrates called to conference with them) engaged to inquire into their opinions. I found it a harder matter to discover than to confute them, they being the most egregious prevaricators that ever men met with.

The excerpt above comes from the part of Farmer's pamphlet that is addressed directly to John Thurloe, whom Farmer describes as 'secretary of state' and a man whose 'shadow' 'is very substantial'. Thurloe was also

Cromwell's spymaster, and here Farmer is clearly trying to remind his correspondent of what he sees as the danger inherent in the inroads made by what he calls the 'northern locusts' on his home turf. The reader will also notice that Farmer implies that the army garrison at Bristol did not really have enough to do: they were doing what we might call 'busy work' 'that they might seem to be necessary'.

Farmer also throws in the phrase 'levelling design', perhaps as an attempt to suggest to Thurloe that the Quakers had the same motives as the Levellers, John Lilburne's group, who were still regarded as a political threat, though their heyday had passed by 1654.

We have seen how many of the most important and enthusiastic early Quaker men, including Richard Hubberthorne and Nayler himself, had been in the army, and Farmer tells us that the under-employed soldiers of the Bristol garrison 'struck in with' the Quaker visitors. It may be that their knowledge of some of the Quakers' service in the parliamentary army made them sympathetic listeners to their preaching. But they were certainly not the only converts in the city.

As we have seen, the aforementioned Dennis Hollister, who ran a prosperous grocery business in the high street, and by 1656 was joint landlord of the White Hart Inn in

Broadstreet, was a recent convert to Quakerism from the Baptist church. He managed to lure twenty of his Baptist brethren to Quakerism, and when John Camm and John Audland arrived in September 1654 he was able to offer them lodging, and a place to meet. Hollister's orchard seems to have been particularly useful for larger meetings, but Camm and Audland were such an instant success in Bristol in those early days that on the first Sunday of their visit they were forced to hold a meeting in a field near the city, called Earlsmead.

Later that day, at the Royal Fort on St Michael's hill, an even bigger meeting took place. Soon Camm was writing of his and Audland's new followers that:

We are with them from six in the morning: they will come to us before we get up: and unto eleven or sometimes one at night they will never be from us. Go into the fields they will follow us, or go into any house, the house will be filled full, so that we cannot tell how we should get from them. The Lord hath subjected them all under us, and they are as fearful to offend us as a child is to offend its loving father.

Burrough and Howgill heard the good news from Bristol, and wrote to George Fox that 'that is a precious city and a gallant people: their net is like to break with fishes, they have caught so much . . . '

One reason why the Quaker message went down so well in Bristol is that the city was already home to a group of Seekers, similar to those who had listened with such attention to George Fox's message in the north-west. Like their northern counterparts, the Bristol Seekers had broken off from the mainstream churches and met together in gatherings remarkably similar to Quaker meetings. As the Lancashire Quaker Richard Clayton wrote to Margaret Fell:

There were many which were seeking after the Lord, and there were a few of us that kept one day of the week in fasting and prayer; so that when this day came we met together early in the morning, not tasting anything; and sat down sometimes in silence, and as any found a concern on their spirits and inclination in their hearts they kneeled down and sought the Lord; so that sometimes, before the day ended, there might be twenty of us might pray, men and women, and sometimes children spake a few words in prayer . . .

No doubt exhausted by all the missionary activity in Bristol, Camm and Audland returned to the north, and Burrough and Howgill took over for a while. After a meeting of over two thousand people, again at the fort, the authorities called the Quaker leaders in to be questioned by local ministers and magistrates, at the end of October 1654 (this is no doubt the meeting Farmer attended where he found the

197

Friends to be 'most egregious prevaricators').

The session was presided over by the mayor, and before the interrogation of the Quakers ended, they were ordered to leave the city. They argued that there was no law that could make them go.

Unable to make the Quakers go away by legal means, in December Friends' enemies recruited King Mob to help out. Ralph Farmer provoked the city's apprentices to riot against the newcomers, and they attacked Camm and Audland (who had now returned to Bristol) on the city's thirteenth-century bridge over the river Avon.

The two men had been attempting to go to a meeting on the other side of the bridge, but the rioters held them back and dragged them off to the medieval Tolzey Court. There Camm and Audland managed to escape into the house of a fellow-Quaker, which the mob threatened to pull down.

Camm had written that in Bristol 'the priests and magistrates of the city begin to rage, but the soldiers keep them down,' and it was members of the garrison who saw off the rioting apprentices. Camm and Audland were saved, and were able to cross the bridge in safety the next morning.

An interesting feature of these anti-quaker riots in Bristol was that the rioters chanted royalist slogans in favour of the king in exile, Charles II. It seems that they had lumped Quakers, Republicans and Puritans all together in their minds.

Ralph Farmer, who had described the Quakers as 'morris-dancers from the north' went on, in his *Great Mysteries,* to revive the idea that they were secretly Roman Catholics: 'they may come upon Antichrist's errand; and not much improbable; for Lancashire and those parts is as famous for Papists as witches'. (Farmer's mention of witches was probably inspired by the aforementioned case of the Pendle Witches.)

The suspicion that the Quakers were indeed 'Papists' in disguise was given official form in January: this was January 1654, as in those days England was still using the old-style calendar, and the new year did not start until the twenty-fifth of March. The Bristol magistrates issued a warrant dated the twenty-fifth of January 1654, stating that 'certain strangers going under the names of John Camm, John Audland, George Fox, James Nayler, and Edward Burrough, and others unknown' were in fact 'persons of the Franciscan order in Rome'. The warrant demanded that 'the constables of the peace' should 'make diligent search throughout your ward for the aforesaid strangers . . . and to apprehend or bring them before us'.

According to Latimer's *Annals of Bristol*, this was a reaction to the ludicrous 'evidence' given by George Cowlishaw, the iron-monger, whose story of Catholic friars disguised as Quakers was also used by Richard Baxter as 'proof' that the Friends were not what they seemed.

The warrant provided anyone in authority in Bristol who was not sympathetic to Quakerism with an excuse to persecute Friends with at least a veneer of legality.

Soon one Thomas Murford was taken out of a meeting and brought before the magistrates, who accused him of being a Franciscan because he was wearing what they regarded as a hair shirt. In fact, Murford was wearing sackcloth because, he claimed, God had told him to do so. Thomas found himself in the city's Newgate prison, and, when his wife complained, she was imprisoned in Bristol's Bridewell (confusingly, London, Bristol and other places had prisons called Newgate and Bridewell at the time).

As if the January 1654 warrant could justify any harsh treatment of Friends, however arbitrary, more were locked up, and/or placed in the stocks, with little or no legal justification.

In May, after the year had changed to 1655, Sarah Goldsmith was thrown into the Bristol Bridewell for walking through the streets in sackcloth and ashes, as were her companions

Anne Cunnicliffe and Margaret Wood.

Like Camm and Audland, Sarah had narrowly escaped violence at the hands of the populace, but others were not so fortunate. John Smith was sorely beaten and his clothes were damaged before he arrived at the Bristol Newgate, and one Elizabeth Marshall received similar treatment. She may have been the 'Mrs Marshall' recorded in Latimer's *Annals*, who was thrust out of a Bristol church in December 1654 and 'received a pelting from the crowd gathered outside', because she had denounced the minister, our friend Ralph Farmer, as a 'dumb shepherd'.

Under these circumstances, tragedies were likely to happen, and indeed two did. One George Harrison died in prison, and a woman called Temperance Hignell was knocked down and beaten after she had criticised a local priest at the end of his sermon, as Elizabeth Marshall had done. It is likely that poor Temperance received a severe blow to the head, 'to the taking away her senses', and she was so ill in prison that she 'was carried out in a basket' and died just a few days later.

Christopher Birkhead was also knocked on the head, but by a priest wielding a stick.

The deaths of George Harrison and Temperance Hignell, and the ecclesiastical violence used on Christopher Birkhead, all happened in Bristol in 1656, the year when Nayler and his companions re-enacted Jesus' entrance into Jerusalem on Palm Sunday, as they entered Bristol through the Ratcliffe Gate.

How had all this persecution of the Quakers happened in a place where, as John Camm had written, 'the priests and magistrates of the city begin to rage, but the soldiers keep them down'?

Clearly, the warrant for the arrest of Quakers on the ludicrous grounds that they were Roman Catholic infiltrators had worked, by motivating long-held prejudices against both Catholics and foreigners, casting shade on the motivations of the Quakers, and giving both the authorities and the populace an excuse to harass them.

In his slimy open letter to Cromwell's spymaster, John Thurloe, included in his 1655 pamphlet *The Great Mysteries*, Ralph Farmer is probably referring to the 1654 warrant when he writes that 'his Highness [meaning Cromwell] . . . hath driven away these northern locusts from us, and given a command for the remove of their abettors & favourites'. Later Farmer asserts that by this action 'his highness hath gained much upon the hearts of our citizens', who were previously 'made [to] believe, these men had countenance from him: which (upon my knowledge) made our magistrates here so backward to be quick with them, and to deal so severely (and justly) with them, as they have been dealt with in other places'.

Another reason for the greater exposure of the Bristol Quakers (and Friends from elsewhere coming into the city) to both official and unofficial persecution was the diminution of the numbers of soldiers garrisoned there. In 1655 Ralph Farmer had hinted that these men had become superfluous by 1654, three years after the end of the civil wars; and plans had been laid to disgarrison the city as early as February 1650. By 1656, so a royalist agent reported, there were only sixty soldiers left in Bristol. The civilian watchmen now policed the city again, and many of the weapons and other items of military equipment once kept there had been removed. Order had also been given for the demolition of the city's castle, and its fort.

The Bristol James Nayler and his followers entered on the twenty-fourth of October 1656 was therefore a very different city from the one Camm and Audland had come to in September 1654. There were no longer troops of sympathetic soldiers poised to protect them, and encourage them by inviting them to hold meetings at their fort. And whereas Camm and Audland had quickly been swamped by sympathetic supporters, so few Bristol Quakers turned out to support Nayler in 1656 that it seems likely that the Friends had been forewarned, and advised to stay at home.

After Nayler was released from prison at Exeter, he set off for London, intending to visit other places, including Bristol, along the way. His travelling companions were a Devon man called Timothy Wedlock, someone called Samuel Cater from the Isle of Ely, a Robert Crab, Hannah Stranger and her husband John, Martha Simmonds, and the Quaker preacher Dorcas Erbury.

Dorcas, a Welsh woman whose mother Mary also became a Quaker preacher, had been with Nayler in prison an Exeter where, she claimed, she had lain dead for two days, but was then miraculously revived by James. By the time she reached Exeter, she had already suffered one imprisonment for her beliefs, at Cardiff, and was thrown into Bristol's Newgate soon after she reached the city with Nayler. This made three imprisonments in one year for poor Dorcas.

Before Nayler's group got to Bristol, they visited Glastonbury, and Bedminster, then a small town to the south of Bristol. At Bedminster, one George Witherly, later a witness to these events in court, advised them that they did not need to go through 'a dirty way' that left them knee-deep in mud.

The mud was there because it was raining

hard, so that, in Witherly's words, Nayler's group 'received the rain at their necks and vented it at their hose and breeches'.

In both Glastonbury and Bedminster, the group had appeared like a re-enactment of Christ's entry to Jerusalem, throwing down their cloaks in front of Nayler's horse, instead of the palm branches that gave Palm Sunday its name. But they were not stopped, arrested or questioned at either of these places.

By the time they got close to Bristol, early in the afternoon, John Stranger was leading the way, while Hannah and Martha were holding the reins of Nayler's horse. Another horse followed, with Dorcas and Samuel Cater riding on it together, while the rest of the party walked alongside Nayler's horse (though some sources say there were three horses altogether). As they proceeded in this way, the women sang, 'Holy, holy, holy, Hosannah', but Witherly, who had followed the group, later complained that the singing had a strange buzzing sound, and he could not make out what they were singing.

A large number of people had turned out to watch them, despite the rain, though they would see few Quakers other than themselves that day. The group, no doubt still muddy, soaked to the skin and singing, proceeded to the city's fourteenth-century High Cross, which then stood right in the centre of town, where Broad

Street, Wine Street, Corn Street and High Street met.

Various important historical events had taken place at the High Cross during Bristol's history, including the execution of traitors in medieval times. From the High Cross, the group proceeded along Broad Street to the White Hart Inn. In a letter to Margaret Fell, the Bristol Quaker George Bishop described the White Hart as 'a bad inn', though, as we know, two Quakers, one of them Dennis Hollister, were the landlords. At the White Hart, some of the curious crowd even followed the Nayler group into their chamber. Bishop describes, with evident distaste, how the women took off some of their upper garments to dry them at the fire, despite the presence of the strangers looking on.

By this time, most of the city must have known about, if not actually seen and heard, Nayler's 'sign', and the authorities reacted by hauling the Friends in for questioning. There were, however, too many people thronging around, and the women would not stop singing, so an attempt at interrogation was abandoned and all seven were thrown into Bristol's Newgate prison for the night.

The next morning, the 'Nayler seven' were questioned in front of the mayor, aldermen and magistrates of Bristol.

A number of local priests were also present

at the hearing, including Ralph Farmer. It is hard to imagine that his face did not bear a look of satisfaction, or at least pleasurable anticipation, at the start of this hearing. Farmer had been against the Quakers from the start, but on some level he must have known that his use of Bristol's apprentices against them was dangerous and irresponsible. It would seem from parts of his pamphlet *The Great Mysteries* that he was also quite aware that the idea that the Friends were secretly Catholic missionaries really wouldn't hold water. In *The Great Mysteries*, he points out similarities between the ideas of the Quakers and those of the Roman Catholics, but he is unable to present any evidence to back up his conspiracy theory.

The questioning of Nayler and his group that Saturday morning promised to be more dangerous to the Friends than Farmer's written accusations, however. There was now a good chance that Nayler at least could be made to look like a blasphemer, within the terms of the 1650 Blasphemy Act then in force. And the court's decision did not need to rely entirely on the evidence of witnesses, and answers given by the accused. A large number of letters, some of them potentially incriminating, had been found on Nayler's person.

XIII. Questions and Answers

The contents of some of the letters found on Nayler are included in Ralph Farmer's pamphlet *Satan Enthroned in his Chair of Pestilence*. The chief reason why these letters could be deployed as evidence of blasphemy was their use of extravagant terms for Nayler. Hannah Stranger wrote that James was the 'everlasting Son of righteousness and Prince of Peace', and the 'fairest of ten thousand, thou only begotten son of God'. In terms that remind one of the eroticism of the Old Testament Song of Songs, Hannah goes on to describe 'how my heart panteth after thee; O stay me with flagons and comfort me with wine'.

The erotic language was not limited to Nayler's female correspondents. A Richard Fairman asserted in one of the letters found on Nayler that 'I am overcome with that love that is as strong as death. O my soul is melting within me, when I beheld thy beauty and innocency, dear and precious son of Zion, whose mother is a virgin, and whose birth is immortal'.

A bold phrase from one of these letters that has been singled out by many authors was also written by a man. In a short postscript added to a letter from Hannah Stranger, her husband John Stranger writes to Nayler that 'thy name is no more to be called James but Jesus'.

Some of the phrases that were applied to Nayler in the letters found on him at Bristol are shocking even today, and they seem calculated to give unsympathetic or even neutral readers the distinct impression that his followers really believed that he was Jesus. Bearing in mind that conventional Christian theology suggests that Jesus and God are the same, anyone reading the letters with a knowledge of the 1650 Blasphemy Act would surely see that Nayler and his correspondents were at risk of being prosecuted under that Act, which was explicitly targeted at any:

who shall presume avowedly in words to profess, or shall by writing proceed to affirm and maintain him or her self, or any other mere creature, to be very God, or to be infinite or almighty, or in honour, excellency, majesty and power to be equal, and the same with the true God

The extravagant terms employed in parts of some of the Bristol letters must, however, be seen in the context of the kind of language often applied by their followers to leadership figures and others in the Quaker movement at the time.

We have already seen how, in her anguished October 1656 letter to Nayler, Margaret Fell referred to George Fox as 'him to whom all nations shall bow' and a name 'to which every knee must bow'. Elsewhere, Fox's followers addressed him as a man 'who art one with the Father,' 'who is dead and alive, and forever lives' and a 'god of life and power'.

Not all the letters found on Nayler at Bristol, which Farmer reproduced, were positive about James, however. A letter from George Fox, written in the handwriting of the Bristol Quaker George Bishop, said that Nayler 'must bear thine own burden, and thy company with thee, whose iniquity doth increase'.

As well as the letters found on Nayler, the search conducted at Bristol discovered a curious little document in the possession of one of the three women. This was a copy of a description of the character and physical appearance of Jesus, supposedly written by one Publius Lentulus, whom Farmer describes as 'president of Judea' during the reign of the Roman emperor Tiberius.

According to Publius, Jesus, 'a man of great virtue', was a tall, handsome individual with long, hazel-coloured hair parted in the middle, that was straight until it reached the ears, but then became wavy. According to this apocryphal fragment, Jesus is also supposed to have had a forked beard of the same colour as his hair.

The Publius Lentulus fragment could be used against Nayler because it was taken as evidence that the Yorkshireman had deliberately changed his appearance so as to look like the Jesus described there. As Farmer writes:

This wretch James Nayler being somewhat fitted for it by bodily shape, colour of his hair, and some other advantages of nature, endeavours artificially to compose and dispose himself, as much [as he may] to this description, parting the hair of his head, cutting his beard forked, assuming an affected gravity, and other the like, as is there expressed.

Like much else in Farmer's writings about the Quakers, his assertion that Nayler already looked like Jesus as described by Publius Lentulus is contradicted in other sources. There are, likewise, other contemporary records of the interrogation of Nayler and his group at Bristol, and these contradict each other on some points.

The overall impression is that when the Nayler seven were interrogated at Bristol, the contents of some of the letters found on James provoked some of the questions put to them. Other questions arose out of the 'blasphemous' sign they were supposed to have enacted the day before. As recorded by Ralph Farmer, Nayler's answers were short and sometimes rather cryptic and evasive, and he responded to some questions with silence.

Asked if he was indeed 'the only begotten son of God,' Nayler replied 'I am the Son of God, and the Son of God is but one'. This was identified by Ronald Matthews in his book *English Messiahs* as the phrase with which Nayler really pinned down his theological position regarding himself and his relationship with Jesus. If, as Christian theology often asserts, Christ is the same as God, who is everywhere and in everybody, and is, as Nayler said, 'but one,' then someone like Nayler, who feels that he has Christ in him, really *is* Christ: anything else diminishes Christ's status. The Christ in Nayler has a claim to full Christhood, much as the water in a lagoon has a claim to be part of the sea.

Even if he had favoured the mayor, aldermen, magistrates and priests of Bristol with a lengthy and well-reasoned explanation of his position, it is unlikely that Nayler would have avoided the further questioning and punishment that awaited him in London. The Bristol authorities saw the Quakers in general, and Nayler in particular, as threatening, destabilising growths, and they were determined to prune them back, whatever fine points of theology were involved.

As well as a range of answers to questions that pertained to Nayler's understanding of himself and his relationship to Jesus, some of Nayler's thinking with regard to his followers emerged from the Bristol hearing. Although he seemed to have an incomplete mental picture of their activities on the road from Exeter to Bristol, Nayler seems to have thought that he could not command them to stop, because he believed that their actions were inspired by the Holy Spirit. Asked why he had ridden into Bristol 'in such an unusual manner' Nayler explained that 'it was for the praises of my Father, and I may not refuse anything that is moved of the Lord'.

In one place in Farmer's record, Nayler tried to deflect a question from himself onto his followers, as if he were reluctant to take responsibility for their actions. Asked to whom their cries of 'holy, holy' were addressed, James responded 'they are of age to answer for themselves'.

Although Nayler was not entirely coherent, or at all comprehensive, in his answers at Bristol, there is no sign that he was insane at this time, though many commentators, particularly in the nineteenth century, insisted that he and some if not all of his followers were quite mad. Farmer's record of the Bristol interrogation is further evidence that, confronted with stress and spiritual uncertainty, the Yorkshireman could retreat into silence or extreme taciturnity; but this was and is part of the temperament of many people, and is certainly not in itself an indicator of insanity. Before his questioners at Bristol, James may also have been afflicted by feelings of fear and uncertainty. No doubt tired and dishevelled after his sodden ride from Exeter, and a night in Bristol's Newgate, he could not have been expected to give of his best.

While Nayler and his followers were being questioned in this way, the Bristol Quaker George Bishop was meeting with other Quakers in the city and, as he wrote to Margaret Fell, 'in silence was the presence of the Lord very great, & the Lord went forth with his power to preserve all his lambs & babes in one'. He meant that the Bristol Quakers were not subjected to another riot, or other forms of confrontation with angry Bristolians provoked by Nayler's 'sign'.

Indeed, Bishop suggests that the position of the Bristol Quakers improved immediately after the 'sign' because even those Bristolians who were previously hostile to Friends could see that the non-Nayler group were something other than enactors of controversial 'signs':

Friends are all kept & preserved; none are hurt, none go to visit them [meaning the Nayler group] (as I can hear of) . . . that of God in the whole town witnessed to us & our innocency . . . & whereas the highest rage might have been expected . . . the priests are cut short of their hopes of striking the truth

While George Bishop and the Bristol Quakers were rejoicing that the local people were able to distinguish between them and the Nayler group, a prominent one-time supporter of Nayler was soon making it clear that he could no longer go along with them.

Readers might have noticed that although Hannah Stranger's husband John, the London comb-maker, formed part of the controversial procession into Bristol, Martha Simmonds' husband Thomas was conspicuous by his absence. In fact he had separated from the group at Exeter, and Ralph Farmer gleefully reproduces a highly critical letter he sent to his wife after he heard about the Bristol 'sign'.

Thomas claimed to have been told by God not to journey to London with the rest of the group via Bristol, but to go directly to the capital. In his letter, he accuses his wife of being 'the chief leader in that action', meaning the Bristol 'sign', and asks her 'if there was such a glory amongst you, why were you not silent, and have let the people cry 'hosanna'?' He identifies the group's central 'problem', as we might say, as an inability to discern when an inner call 'to speak or act' comes from God, or 'from the earthly dark principle'. 'Hence,' Thomas continues, 'comes all your cumber and trumpery without'.

Rejected by many of their own sect, and even criticised by the husband of one of them; far from home and with only enemies to listen to them, the Nayler group must have felt very isolated and vulnerable as they waited to hear what the Bristol authorities would decide to do with them.

It was decided that some of Nayler's group should be sent to London to be questioned by parliament itself. As well as James, Hannah and John Stranger, Martha Simmonds and Dorcas Erbury were to go. According to the *Annals of Bristol*, the corporation paid four pounds and ten shillings for the hire of horses to get them to the capital, and the government paid the other expenses, amounting to thirty-seven pounds, or about three thousand pounds at today's values (although the Speaker of the House of Commons later complained that the transfer of the prisoners had cost twenty-six pounds).

In London, the 'Nayler five', as they now were, were accommodated at a house in Westminster that Richard Hubberthorne, who visited them there, described as an inn. Bittle tells us that it belonged to one of the men who escorted them from Bristol. In a letter to

Margaret Fell, Hubberthorne described how 'Parliament men' visited the group there, to question Nayler and the others about their beliefs and actions. James sometimes put these people off 'without giving them a full answer and left them unsatisfied'. Many others, both Quakers and non-Quakers, also dropped by. Hubberthorne told Fell that 'the women are exceedingly filthy' (meaning sinful), that they were possessed by 'a power of darkness' and that they acted 'in imitations', sang, howled and knelt before James. Hubberthorne tried to convince Nayler that he should discourage this behaviour, but as at Bristol the prisoner insisted that the behaviour was inspired by God. Hubberthorne left with a feeling of pity for Nayler in his heart, and a bleak hope that:

at the end of the days of the imitation it will fall to the earth again. And the sun will shine over it. And the children will receive power of the son to reign over all deceit.

On November the fifteenth, the Nayler five were called before a specially-assembled committee of fifty-five men who questioned them in the Painted Chamber of the Palace of Westminster.

The Painted Chamber was a reminder that many spaces in the palace that were then used for parliamentary business had originally been built as rooms for a royal palace. The Painted Chamber, an exceptionally long, narrow and high room, had been built in the thirteenth century, and served at first as a private apartment for King Henry III. Its name was derived from the brightly-coloured murals that adorned its walls. These featured battle scenes, biblical scenes, symbolic figures and a depiction of the coronation of Edward the Confessor. The pictures had been whitewashed over by 1799: it is unclear whether they would have been visible when Nayler was questioned in the chamber in 1656. Rather ominously, the Chamber, which stood between the rooms then used by the House of Commons and the House of Lords respectively, had been used as a place to hear evidence during the trial of Charles I.

The hearings of the Nayler committee were well-attended, perhaps because James's case had become famous, if not notorious, and many people with a right to attend did not want to miss the chance to see the man himself, and to hear his words and those of his followers. Later, when the case was debated in the House of Commons next door, a Major Beake reminded the House that there had been 'almost 150 there'. In the same debate, Thomas Bampfield said he believed that 'most of the House were there,' which suggests that one hundred and fifty might have been a conservative estimate.

Bampfield knew about the committee that

questioned the Nayler group in the Painted Chamber, because he had chaired it. Thomas was a staunch Presbyterian, a convinced Republican, a formidable legal mind and a leading man down in Exeter, where Nayler and his friends had been imprisoned. The proceedings of the committee were recorded by, among others, William Grigge, the Bristol man who had clashed with his fellow Bristolian Dennis Hollister about the new Quaker sect. Grigge's record cannot be regarded as accurate, unbiased or even complete: like all the surviving records relating to Nayler's life, it has to be handled with care.

In his *The Quaker's Jesus*, Grigge offers 'an account briefly of [Nayler's] examinations in London' which, despite Grigge's anti-Quaker bias, is not terribly incriminating.

In the Painted Chamber, according to Grigge's record, Nayler was less evasive than he had been when questioned at Bristol: he deflected fewer of the questions put to him, and refused to answer questions only when they were in effect repetitions of questions he had already answered. Once again, we get the impression that, perhaps because he was stressed or preoccupied, he really couldn't remember certain details of what had happened to him, and what had been said to him and about him, between his departure from Exeter and his arrest at Bristol.

Nayler claimed that he could not exactly remember if his followers had chanted 'holy, holy,' or whether the bridle of his horse had been held by women or men, or if anyone had kissed his feet when he was in prison.

As at Bristol, Nayler asserted that he could not stop the adoring way that some of his followers behaved towards him, because, when he did question them about it, they said they 'were moved of the Lord to it'. Before Bampfield's committee, he gave a more detailed account of the theology of how he saw himself in relation to Jesus, than he had at Bristol. Now he asserted that he believed he was indeed the son of God, but he added that he had 'many brethren'. He was Jesus, to the extent that the spirit dwelt in him, but this was a purely spiritual thing: he was not Christ come again in the flesh.

Nayler also indicated that his questioner or questioners could not themselves understand the mysteries and theological distinctions he was referencing. Asked to answer on his relationship to the Virgin Mary, the Yorkshireman said 'there is a womb that you know not of,' reinforcing the idea that he, Nayler, had undergone a second, spiritual birth. Asked if he called himself 'King of Israel', James told his interrogator that Christ 'hath a kingdom, of which thou wottest [knoweth] not'.

Here as elsewhere in his spoken and written statements, Nayler referred to the 'measure' of Christ within him, suggesting that he could accept that it was in some way limited, but was perhaps more plentiful in him than in many other people. Asked if there was 'worship due to you, which was to Christ?' he answered that 'if they did it to the visible, they were to blame, but if to the invisible, that worship is due to me, according to my measure, as was due to Christ'.

Again, as at Bristol, there is no sense here that Nayler was mad. Considering the threat and stress he was under, and that he was a prisoner being questioned by a body many of whom would have liked to see him hanged, James's answers were remarkably consistent and coherent. Indeed, the only disorderly element in the session as reported by Grigge was the tendency of the questioners to ask the same question twice, but in different words; for instance the question 'do you own that attribute of being the only begotten Son of God?' immediately followed by the question 'are you the only begotten Son of God?'

According to Judge Anthony Pearson, Nayler achieved rather more at his hearing than merely showing that he was not mad, answering questions in a coherent manner and recognising when he was being asked the same question twice. Pearson, who had also, of course, been very impressed by Nayler's performance under questioning at Appleby, wrote that before the committee:

James answered all the accusations with so much wisdom & meekness, & clearness to the understanding of all indifferent persons, that the whole assembly except some violent men of the committee was strangely astonished & satisfied with his answer . . .

Pearson's words are one of a number of hints preserved in the records that Nayler may have come over as impressive – something of a formidable character – during his appearances at the Palace of Westminster. In a way, his composure made his situation more precarious. Under the Blasphemy Act of 1650, offenders could not be prosecuted under the Act if they were 'distempered with sickness, or distracted in brain'.

XIV. More Questions Than Answers

Bampfield's committee was charged with drawing up a report that could be presented to the House of Commons, which it did in the form of a fifteen-page document that Bampfield read out near the start of the debate on the guilt or innocence of the man from West Ardesley.

In those days, before most of the medieval Palace of Westminster burned down in 1834, the House of Commons met in St Stephen's Chapel, which had stopped being a place of worship over a hundred years before Nayler's extremely unusual trial. At around ninety-five by thirty feet, the chamber was a little wider than a modern tennis court, though somewhat longer.

The room retained the basic layout of a medieval English chapel, such as can still be found among the buildings of old university colleges, and the country seats of great families. The members of parliament sat in two blocks, facing each other, as if they were in the choir of a medieval cathedral. The Speaker's chair was on a raised stone dais at one end, and at the other was a public gallery, reached, not by a staircase of any kind, but by a ladder.

The space could easily become overcrowded, so it is not surprising that one of the members once tried to sit on the ladder itself. On this occasion, the Speaker complained that the member looked as if he were waiting to be hanged.

The layout of St Stephen's Chapel is still reflected in the design of the modern chamber of the House of Commons, which is not much bigger. The fact that the MPs still sit in two blocks, facing each other, is thought by some to encourage confrontational party politics: MPs must literally choose a side. In many more modern parliamentary chambers, the members sit in a circle, or parts of a circle: in the Scottish parliament in Edinburgh, for instance, members sit in a fan-shape, which gives the impression that, despite their party differences, they are at least pointing in roughly the same direction.

Although they met in a room that was later lauded as the setting for some remarkable democratic breakthroughs, the parliament that sat in judgement on James Nayler was not the product of popular, untrammelled democracy, and it was neither free nor independent.

At that time, the House of Commons had to

work alongside Oliver Cromwell (then styled 'Lord Protector'), his powerful Council of State, and the major-generals he had imposed on the various regions. Of the major-generals, no less than eight spoke in the Nayler debate, including John Lambert and John Desborough. Both Desborough and Lambert were members of the Council of State as well as major-generals, as were two other major-generals who spoke: Charles Fleetwood and Philip Skippon. Members of the Council who spoke, who were not also major-generals, included Sir Gilbert Pickering and William Sydenham. Near the end of the debate, there were contributions from John Thurloe, Cromwell's spymaster.

It is hardly surprising that so many contributions originated from men who were close to Cromwell, or to whom he had shown favour. When this Second Protectorate Parliament, as it was called, attempted to sit for the first time, around a hundred of them were prevented from doing so by the Council of State. Outraged by this offence to democracy, fifty more members refused to sit, so that in the end only two hundred and fifty, or around sixty percent of the members elected, took their seats.

Cromwell had called the parliament partly to raise money for his army and his major-generals, and also to help fund the Anglo-Spanish war that, according to Cromwell's biographer S.R. Gardiner, the Lord Protector had started almost by accident, because he was unable to grasp the international situation at the time. Also according to Gardiner, it is possible that the Second Protectorate Parliament chewed over Nayler's case for so long because they were trying to avoid debating the Militia Bill, the passing of which would have released the funds Cromwell wanted.

The length of the debates over Nayler, which stretched over an astonishing eleven days, prompted the Victorian writer Thomas Carlyle to describe them as 'interminable . . . excelling in stupor all the human speech, even in English parliaments, this editor has ever been exposed to'.

Carlyle had to read over the record of the debate, albeit reluctantly, because he was preparing his edition of Cromwell's letters and speeches at the time. He goes on to say of the debate that 'nowhere does the unfathomable deep of dullness which our English character has in it, more stupendously disclose itself'.

The record Carlyle complained about so bitterly was a partial transcript preserved in the diary of Thomas Burton, an undistinguished member of parliament who, if he spoke at all in the Nayler debate, did not mention it in his diary. As MP for Westmorland, in some ways the home of Quakerism, Nayler's case may have had a special interest for Burton, though he admits that he did not attend every minute of the relevant debates.

The reason why the debates are tedious, or at least repetitive, is because, although some of the men who contributed were among the most powerful in the land, the atmosphere of these sessions, as recorded by Burton, is an atmosphere of uncertainty. If the members were not merely filibustering, then their repeated failure to find a conclusion to their deliberations was surely bred out of the fact that they were unsure as to how to proceed.

A major stumbling-block, at least in the early days of the debates, was the fact that, under normal circumstances, the House of Commons cannot sit as a court of law. Until recently the House of Lords had a judicial function, but their lordships' house had been abolished with the establishment of the commonwealth in 1649, when it was declared that the country 'shall from henceforth be governed as a commonwealth and free-state . . . without any king or House of Lords'.

There was also a great deal of uncertainty about what type of crime Nayler was supposed to have committed: was it blasphemy or 'horrid blasphemy'? What had he done or said that made him guilty of blasphemy? Was he not 'really bewitched'? Might not the precedent of punishing Nayler for blasphemy set off a disastrous string of further blasphemy trials, for instance of the Jews and Turks (meaning Muslims) who were then living in Britain?

Many of those members of the Second Protectorate Parliament who agreed that they should do something about James Nayler were unsure whether they should pass sentence in the form of an Act of Parliament, or directly, as a court of law would usually do.

There was also a great deal of debate about what sentence should be passed down: the House narrowly voted against executing Nayler, but before that, stoning Nayler to death, a punishment that regularly features in the Bible, was seriously suggested, and by several members. The grisly procedure of hanging, drawing and quartering was also proposed, for instance by Major-General Skippon.

Once the danger of judicial execution had passed, the idea of cutting out Nayler's tongue and removing his right hand were seriously entertained, as was the idea of slitting his lips. Banishment was also considered, Britain's new colony of Jamaica being among the places suggested for Nayler's exile: other places proposed included Scotland, the Orkney Islands and 'Biddle in the Isle of Scilly'.

Although many were unsure what to do with him and how to do it, a number of the honourable members were agreed that Nayler was a truly wicked man. Whereas his followers had called him 'the fairest of ten thousand', Nathaniel Bacon called him 'the foulest of ten thousand', while other members called him leper, antichrist, idolater, imposter, seducer, viper and wolf, among other epithets.

Many members were confident enough when it came to calling names, but the atmosphere of uncertainty thickened again when the Speaker, Thomas Widdrington, MP for Northumberland, suffered a sort of panic attack before Nayler was due to be called up to be sentenced:

What shall I say to him? Shall I ask him any questions? or, if he speak, what shall I answer? Shall I barely pronounce the sentence, and make no preamble to it? I can do nothing but by your directions. I pray you inform me.

At last, Widdrington pronounced the sentence. As recorded in the record of the Commons' vote, Nayler was to:

be set on the pillory with his head in the pillory in the Palace yard, Westminster, during the space of two hours on Thursday next, and shall be whipped by the hangman through the streets from Westminster to the Old Exchange, London; and there likewise be set on the pillory with his head in the pillory for the space of two hours, between the hours of eleven and one on Saturday next, in each place wearing a paper containing an inscription of his crimes; and that at the Old Exchange his tongue be bored through with a hot iron, and that he be there also stigmatised in the forehead with the letter B; and that he be afterwards sent to Bristol, and be conveyed into and through the said city on horseback, bare-ridged [bareback], with his face backward, and there also publicly whipped the next market-day after he comes thither; and that from thence he be committed to prison in Bridewell, London, and there restrained from the society of all people, and there to labour hard, till he shall be released by Parliament; and during that time be debarred the use of pen, ink and paper, and shall have no relief but what he earns by his daily labours.

The letter 'B' was of course to stand for 'Blasphemer'. The idea of setting the prisoner to hard labour was mentioned in the Commons debates by a Mr Robinson, who suggested that 'it is idleness has brought the fellow to these high notions; whereas hard labour will bring him to sleep, and consequently to settlement again'. This early theory of occupational therapy reminds one of Thomas Baxter's belief that if only he could 'plough and dig,' he 'should yet hope to live in some competent health'.

Throughout the Nayler debates in the House of Commons, the honourable members referred to those of James's followers who were imprisoned with him as 'the women' although one of the four, John Stranger, was a man.

Some argued that 'the women' were more guilty than Nayler, because they had turned him into an idol, and thus become idolaters. The implication here is that James's followers thought that he may have had more of God or Jesus in him than he himself claimed in his evidence given to the Bampfield committee and to the Commons. At the end of the day's proceedings on the seventeenth of December, when Nayler had been sentenced, and on the next day, the question arose as to what should be done with Martha Simmonds and the rest.

William Sydenham, a member of the Council of State, was surprised to find that, having sentenced Nayler to such a harsh punishment, the House seemed disinclined to sentence 'the women':

. . . how zealous they were for that high sentence against Nayler, though there was no law at all for it, and never quiet till it was done; and now, how different. A punishment far lesser would content them against these women; who, in my opinion, were greater offenders than Nayler, inasmuch as they actually committed idolatry.

It is not clear exactly what happened to 'the women' next, but they appear to have been

231

released fairly quickly.

Sydenham's words were part of a debate held on the eighteenth of December 1656, which followed on from the debates about Nayler and was an attempt to find a solution to the 'Quaker threat' in general. On the same day, Nayler was undergoing the first phase of his punishment in the bitter cold outside.

As if three hundred and ten strokes with knotted cords were not enough, the Yorkshire Quaker William Tomlinson reported that 'the bailiffs that rid as the cart went on along were very cruel; some of them trod many times on his feet with their horses, and crushed him against the cart.' Nevertheless Tomlinson tells us that 'yet opened he not his mouth, nor doth a harsh word come out of his mouth, against them that hath thus used him, but prays for them, sometimes with tears'.

Rebecca Travers, who had been converted from the Baptist faith by Nayler, tended James's wounds in Newgate prison and stated that there:

was not the space of a man's nail free from stripes and blood, from his shoulders, near to his waist, his right arm sorely striped, his hands much hurt with cords, that they bled and were swelled; the blood and wounds of his back did very little appear at first sight, by reason of abundance of dirt that covered them, till it was washed off

Some Members of Parliament had been concerned that a severe form of corporal punishment might kill Nayler, which may be one reason why they were receptive to a petition asking that 'an order of reprieve may be granted for a few days, and it will be accepted as an act of your Christian moderation and clemency'.

As a result of the petition, the second part of Nayler's punishment was delayed until Saturday the twenty-seventh of December. Despite a further petition begging Parliament to cancel the second part of the punishment altogether, James was still branded on the forehead, and his tongue bored through, on that day.

John Deacon, who was a witness of the punishment, reported that Martha Simmonds, Hannah Stranger and Dorcas Erbury mounted the scaffold and arranged themselves around the pillory where Nayler was strapped in, in imitation of the three Marys who stood at the base of the cross of Jesus in John 19: 25: 'Now there stood by the cross of Jesus his mother, and his mother's sister, Mary the wife of Cleophas, and Mary Magdalene'.

Robert Rich, a fanatical supporter of Nayler who had not been involved in the Bristol incident, stuck a paper over Nayler's head that read 'this is the king of the Jews'. A little later, when Nayler's forehead was branded, Rich licked the wound.

William Tomlinson was close enough to Nayler when his forehead was branded to see a puff of smoke go up when the brand was applied. He evidently did not get a good view of the hot iron used to bore Nayler's tongue, but reported that 'some say it was great, near the bigness of a tobacco pipe, and it was thrust a great way through'. Tomlinson also reported that Nayler 'did not move nor shrink all the while they did these things to him.'

More whipping was carried out at Bristol, where Nayler was forced to retrace the steps he took during the Bristol 'sign' while seated bare-back, and facing backwards, on a horse. Eventually, he ended up in London's Bridewell Prison, where he had been sentenced to remain until Parliament saw fit to release him. There he was to be set to hard labour, and not to receive any food unless he had earned it by his work.

According to Bittle, the work Nayler was put to was hemp-processing, or what used to be called 'picking oakum'. This was a notoriously unpleasant task that involved recycling old hemp ropes by pulling out the fibres to make oakum, a mixture of hemp fibres and tar that was used as a sealant, for instance on ships and water-pipes. Picking oakum was hard on the hands, particularly the fingers, and was generally so unpleasant as a job that it was forced on prisoners like Nayler and, later, on the unfortunate occupants of workhouses.

At first Nayler refused this work, and was consequently denied food. After three days he began to pick oakum, and was fed. Pickers of oakum were usually paid by the weight of what they produced, and Nayler was duly paid nine pence for every twenty-five pounds. With this sum, equivalent to about three pounds sterling today, Nayler was able to buy food.

Although the prisoner was supposed to be 'restrained from the society of all people' his wife Anne was allowed to visit him in January. Following her visit, his cell was thoroughly searched in order to check that she had not smuggled in pen and paper.

Anne was uneasy about her husband's health, and the conditions he was being kept under. She appealed to Parliament to let her visit him more regularly, and bring him food. Nayler's health problems at this time may have been exacerbated by his habit of fasting: according to the prison authorities, he had been refusing meat and ale.

Although the aptly named prison physician, Dr Nurse, pronounced James fit at the end of February, he was soon declining again, and Nurse reported that the 'cough was increasing upon him, to which he hath been formerly subject in the army'. The possibility that Nayler himself identified this to Dr Nurse as the same type of cough he had had in the army could be evidence that James had indeed been suffering from recurring symptoms of tuberculosis. It is entirely consistent with this disease that it should have returned at times of stress, or when the patient had undergone a change of environment.

Although Nayler had previously been accused of adultery by his critics, it was decided to move him into the cell of one Joan Pollard, a female prisoner at Bridewell. Described as an 'ancient widow', it was no doubt assumed that Joan would be of no interest, sexually, to the ailing Quaker. Joan nursed her new cell-mate, and his health improved.

Though it turned out to have been a good idea, this business of putting a male and a female prisoner together in one cell so that one could nurse the other through an illness is more evidence of the haphazard way that the justice system, and particularly prisons, were run at this time. More evidence of this appears in the records of Nayler's time at Bridewell, in the form of reports of visits from fellow-Quakers, including Hubberthorne, Audland and the Lancashire Quaker Alexander Parker.

By some means or other, by the summer of 1658 Nayler was using ink and paper, which had been explicitly denied to him in the sentence handed down by the House of Commons. He wrote from prison in order to condemn his one-time followers, who were continuing to disrupt Quaker meetings.

No time-limit had been set to Nayler's imprisonment: he was supposed to be waiting until Parliament decided to release him. He may have thought that he would be released if the parliament that had sentenced him collapsed, but given that some seventeenth-century parliaments had endured for a long time (the so-called Long Parliament had earned its nickname by sitting, off and on, for twenty years) James may have suspected, in his darker moments, that he would never leave Bridewell alive.

But as we have seen, the Second Protectorate Parliament, which had tried Nayler in its early days, was always in a tricky position, trying to weigh its independence against the power of Cromwell; and the Protector dissolved it on the fourth of February 1658. Oliver had tried to impose a second House on this parliament, to replace the abolished House of Lords; the replacement second chamber to be populated by his own nominees. The Republicans would not have it, and the House of Commons was shut down.

Oliver Cromwell died on the third of

September 1658, and was succeeded by his son Richard. The Third Protectorate Parliament, with its second chamber, survived for less than three months in 1659, and poor Richard ruled as Protector for only two hundred and sixty-four days. His rapid fall meant that he earned the nick-name 'Tumble-down Dick'. Soon after the collapse of the Third Protectorate Parliament, a number of incarcerated Quakers, including James Nayler, were released.

XV. The Penitent

One of the most important sources for James Nayler's life used in this book is the *Impartial Relation* or *Account* published by the Westmorland Quaker George Whitehead in 1716. Whitehead's *Account* forms the preface to his collection of Nayler's writings, called *A Collection of Sundry Books, Epistles and Papers Written by James Nayler*. Whitehead, who had been a friend of Nayler's, was able to publish this book over fifty years after James's death because he, Whitehead, was twenty years younger than Nayler, and was fortunate enough to live to be nearly ninety years old. After his *Collection* was published, Whitehead lived for another seven years.

As we have seen, Whitehead's *Impartial Relation* tends to cast shade on the activities of Nayler's closest followers in the 1650s, especially the women. Whether George still harboured a dislike for these Friends so long after the events is unclear: what is clear is that the *Impartial Relation* is an apology for Nayler's life – an attempt to rehabilitate his reputation and restore him to a place in the pantheon of Quaker saints.

Directly after his biography of his friend at the start of the *Collection*, Whitehead includes a number of papers written by Nayler 'taken out of his own handwriting', which reflect his state of mind while he was in Bridewell Prison, and after he was released. These papers comprise a series of heart-felt confessions, refutations of some untruths spoken about the author, condemnations of the actions of his one-time disciples, recantations of his former views, and expressions of profound gratitude for those Quakers who had welcomed him back into the fold after he was released from Bridewell. Nayler begs the reader to forgive him for his wicked folly, puts some of the blame on Satan 'whose work it is to sow dissension', and warns the reader not to fall into the trap that caught him.

Whitehead no doubt put these *Papers of Confessions* as he calls them near the front of his *Collection* to melt the hearts of potential readers, particularly Quakers, who might still be thinking of Nayler as a reprobate, a creator of unfortunate situations, an embarrassment, and a man best forgotten. Here, Nayler's editor seems to be saying, is a true penitent, deserving your love and prayers.

In the *Papers*, Nayler denies that he ever committed adultery with his female followers, and also denies that he had 'raised Dorcas Erbury from death . . . though that power that quickens the dead I deny not'.

James expresses himself willing to do anything, 'that all breaches may be removed from the just'. He condemns 'those unclean spirits gone out from the unity of truth' and their 'wild actings', with whom he was 'led captive under the power of darkness' 'in the day when my judgement was taken away'. He accuses those who continue to disrupt Quaker meetings in his name of being 'unclean ranting spirits', having 'the old spirit of the Ranters, which now in a new way makes head against the light of Christ'.

This seems to be a different Quaker from the man who faced branding, whipping and mutilation so bravely, and who tried to interrupt Speaker Bampfield while he was sentencing him, to ask him what crime he, Nayler, was supposed to have committed. Is this the same Nayler who, though under hostile questioning from Bampfield, challenged Parliament itself with the words:

I am set up as a sign to this nation, to bear witness of his coming. You have been a long time under dark forms, neglecting the power of godliness, as bishops. It was the desire of my soul, all along, and the longing expectation of many godly men engaged with you, that this nation should be redeemed from such forms. God hath done it for you, and hath put his sword in the hands of those from whom it cannot be wrested. That sword cannot be broken, unless you break it yourselves, by disobeying the voice, the call, and rejecting the sign set up amongst you to convince them that Christ is come.

It seems that in isolation in prison, where, as is hinted at in the *Papers of Confessions*, his feverish condition may have brought on visions of a spiritual character, Nayler began to long to join what had become main-stream Quakerism, and to distance himself from some of his former disciples. Addressing his new friends among the Friends, he emphasises the importance of humility and submission, for instance in a piece beginning 'Glory to God Almighty', written in 1659:

Art thou in darkness? mind it not, for if thou do it will fill thee more, but stand still and act not, and wait in patience till light arise out of darkness to lead thee.

Although he recommended this almost Zen-like habit of mind to fellow-Quakers, Nayler's old fire reasserted itself after his release when he addressed non-Quakers and anti-Quakers, even among the highest in the land.

Some historians convey the impression that, his health broken, Nayler collapsed into a state of feeble penitence and, as it were, withered away after his time in Bridewell. But as in the time before the Bristol incident, in 1660 Nayler again took up his pen and engaged in pamphlet war.

In May 1660 King Charles II landed at Dover, and proceeded to reclaim the kingdom that had been wrested from his family by Parliament after the execution of his father. Almost before he had his feet firmly under the table as king, he was inundated with advice, some of it in written form. At the end of July, Richard Blome published a pamphlet that was intended as an open letter to the new king. As was often the case at this time, the long title (given here in part) acted as an equivalent of the modern blurb: *The Fanatic History, or an exact relation and account of the Old Anabaptists and New Quakers . . . which may prove the death and burial of the Fanatic doctrine.*

In his *Fanatic History,* Blome, an enterprising publisher, accused the Quakers of all sorts of crimes, including heresy and blasphemy. Hoping, perhaps, that if the king had read Blome's book, he might read his *Short Answer* to it, Nayler responded with all his old energy and focus.

Some of the people Blome accused of

giving the Quakers a bad name were not Quakers at all, Nayler asserted. And the genuine Quakers did not hold the heretical views on religion that Blome accused them of. Blome should not be trying to persuade King Charles to persecute the Quakers – he should be using 'spiritual weapons' if he wants to do battle with the Friends. And in any case, monarchs should treasure their subjects, not persecute them.

In the *Short Answer* to Blome's book, parts of which were written by Richard Hubberthorne, Nayler shows that he is aware of a weakness in his own argument, as he was once the perpetrator of one of the outré 'signs' Blome objects to. James tries to turn this weakness into a strength by implying that it is in the nature of God's people to be tested and corrected by him:

God will not cast off his people, though he be sometimes provoked to correct them, even before their adversaries (which is a sign to them), yet is his anger but for a moment, and his favour shall return as streams of life. Then shall the food be taken out of the mouth of the viper, and the prey from between the teeth of the devourers . . .

Nayler classifies Blome's book with the words of the hypocrites of the 1660 Restoration, who tried to cuddle up to Charles but also seemed to admire Cromwell when it was convenient to do so:

These also were of them that said Oliver Cromwell was Moses, who had led them into a sight of the good land, and that Richard his son was Joshua

As well as the obscure Blome, at this time Nayler also addressed some of the most powerful people in the country through his writing, in an attempt to influence the government to move in the right direction. His *Warning to the Rulers*, published in 1659, is an impassioned plea for religious toleration, and reminds the said rulers that 'it is not merely the name of a king nor of a bishop, by which the innocent people of God have suffered, but by that lordly, oppressing, cruel spirit, and corrupt ordinances . . .'

That Nayler was collaborating with Hubberthorne, once one one of his sternest critics, shows the extent to which he was again a trusted Quaker minister. He continued to speak in public for the Quaker cause, particularly in London where he preached at the house of one William Woodcock in the Strand. Here he attracted such large crowds of newcomers that regular attenders were asked to meet somewhere else. It is possible that if James had not attempted to travel home to Wakefield in the October of 1660 he would have lived and worked in the bosom of

Quakerism well into the reign of the new king.

But a journey of over two hundred and fifty miles, on foot, in one of the winter months, in the midst of the so-called Little Ice Age, was probably not a wise idea when the traveller had recently been so ill, and was also in the habit of fasting. At Huntingdon, sixty-six miles north of London, Nayler was seen by a local Quaker 'in such an awful frame [of mind] as if he had been redeemed from the earth and a stranger on it, seeking a better country and inheritance'. The anonymous Friend's testimony about Nayler's apparent state at this time might, however, have been coloured by his knowledge of what happened next.

Nayler might still have made it to Wakefield, or perhaps returned safely to London, after a short rest at Huntingdon. But the roads were dangerous in those days, for reasons other than frozen paths, penetrating winds and the dangers of exhaustion. Thieves lay in wait to rob travellers, and those who travelled alone and on foot were particularly vulnerable.

Nayler was found one evening, tied up in a field outside Huntingdon, having been beaten and robbed. The details of his physical state after this experience are obscure, but Thomas Parnell, a local Quaker doctor, could do nothing for him, and he died as October drew to a close.

He was buried on the twenty-first of what he would have called Eighth Month, at King's Ripton, Huntingdonshire. His last words, which seem to have been written down by a bedside amanuensis, and perhaps polished a little before publication, are among the most perfect statements of the inner spiritual life ever expressed by a Quaker:

There is a spirit which I feel that delights to do no evil nor to revenge any wrong, but delights to endure all things, in hope to enjoy its own in the end. Its hope is to outlive all wrath and contention, and to weary out all exaltation and cruelty, or whatever is of a nature contrary to itself. It sees to the end of all temptations. As it bears no evil in itself, so it conceives none in thoughts to any other. If it be betrayed, it bears it, for its ground and spring is the mercies and forgiveness of God. Its crown is meekness, its life is everlasting love unfeigned; and takes its kingdom with entreaty and not with contention, and keeps it by lowliness of mind. In God alone it can rejoice, though none else regard it, or can own its life. It's conceived in sorrow, and brought forth without any to pity it, nor doth it murmur at grief and oppression. It never rejoiceth but through sufferings: for with the world's joy it is murdered. I found it alone, being forsaken. I have fellowship therein with them who lived in dens and desolate places in the earth, who through death obtained this resurrection and eternal holy life.

The fact that, in 1659 and 1660, James Nayler

openly and sincerely repented of his actions in 1656, does not necessarily mean that those actions amounted to crimes, either spiritual or in terms of the then laws of the land. As we have seen, the parliamentarian William Sydenham was quite clear that there was 'no law' by which Nayler had been tried and punished, and many hostile members of parliament and others were shocked by the severity of Nayler's sentence, especially given the slight legal justification for it. We know that Nayler himself was unsure what crime he was being prosecuted for, even after eleven days of debate in the House of Commons.

Like much in Nayler's story, the question of his guilt, innocence, folly or madness comes back to the 'Bristol incident': an incident that was and is always open to interpretation, hostile or sympathetic. The incident was not inherently wicked, except in the eye of the beholder. It is sometimes forgotten that Nayler's group rode into both Glastonbury and Bedlington, in a manner likely to suggest Jesus's ride on Palm Sunday, before they reached Bristol. In both of those places, they were allowed to continue unmolested. At Bristol, they found themselves up against a local establishment that was concerned about the recent growth of Quakerism in their city, and whose fears were being whipped up by the unscrupulous Ralph Farmer. The Bristolians were willing and able to put the worst possible interpretation on the 'sign': they were more than ready to do so, and also to exploit their interpretation for their own ends.

The lack of Quaker support the group met with at Bristol was a function of the then split in the Quaker ranks. While George Fox, Margaret Fell and their followers turned their backs on the Nayler group, Martha Simmonds and the others found themselves isolated and vulnerable.

There was really no practical reason for Bristol to send the Nayler group to London: it is as if the authorities in both cities were determined to stage a very public show-trial as a warning to the Quakers, and as a display of their own strength. Like many such trials throughout history, Nayler's misfired: over eleven days, many members of the Second Protectorate Parliament made themselves contemptible by showing themselves to be indecisive, prejudiced, Bible-thumping wind-bags.

The Nayler case does not reflect well on many of James's fellow-Quakers either. It is possible that, like the Speaker of the House of Commons, George Fox felt somewhat intimidated by James Nayler. An older man, with perhaps a superior education (or at least a superior command of written English), Nayler's

249

success as a preacher, particularly in London, may have made Fox feel that James might become the *de facto* leader of the Quakers, at a time when he, Fox, may have been thinking that it was time to take on more of a leadership role himself.

As a result, Fox does not seem to have been as willing to support Nayler in his troubles as a truly confident leader might have done; and when various Friends were winning themselves places in Heaven by trying to reconcile the two men, it was sometimes Fox who was the most stiff and unbending.

From the psychological perspective, it seems unlikely that the two men could have competed for the same role, at least in terms of personality types. Nayler; older, more worldly and experienced, with a powerful potential for a distinctive type of personal, political and spiritual indignation, was really quite unlike George Fox.

At this time, Margaret Fell's powerful devotion to Fox may have tempted her to think of Nayler as a soul on its way to being lost, or at least a disruptive element, rather than as a spiritual comrade who needed support.

In her book *Print Culture and the Early Quakers*, Kate Peters does not hesitate to assert that attempts by rival Quakers to suppress the Nayler group may have stemmed in part from male Quakers' unease about women taking such a dominant role; being so active, independent and outspoken. Peters goes further, and suggests that the organisational changes made among the Quakers at this time were designed, in part, to keep Quaker women under control.

Modern Quakers of both genders would be shocked to see such prejudice in operation in their meetings, but this attitude was not inconsistent with contemporary Quaker views of the roles of the sexes. Many felt that women could be spiritually equal with men, since, among other things, they were just as likely to go to heaven, but inferior when it came to many matters outside of the spiritual realm.

George Whitehead's attempt to revive the reputation of his old friend on the basis of his extant writings was a noble act, though George was guilty of editing parts of these papers, and suppressing others, to soften the overall impact. Although slightly blunted in places by Whitehead's cautious editing, the *Collection of Sundry Books, Epistles, and Papers* reflects the editor's understanding that Nayler's writings had the power to convince, should not be lost, and reflected well on their controversial author.

Whitehead wished to present his friend as a penitent worthy of praise, but sometimes the judgement of history, or at least of historians (both Quakers and non-Quakers) has been

251

extremely harsh on James Nayler. Some have implied that his actions, particularly in Bristol in October 1656, were so reprehensible that they caused a revolution in the Quaker movement, which quickly changed its tone, locked down its procedures and strengthened its organisation precisely so that no more Bristol incidents would occur.

As we have seen, in the nineteenth century, several commentators assumed that James was merely temporarily mad, despite ample evidence to the contrary.

In the opinion of this biographer, James Nayler was not a blasphemer, a heretic, a sower of discord, a fool or a madman, but a genuine Quaker prophet who found himself in the wrong place at the wrong time.

Select Bibliography

Ackroyd, Peter: *Civil War: The History of England Volume III*, Pan, 2015

Ashley, Maurice: *England in the Seventeenth Century*, Penguin, 1958

Baxter, Richard: *The Autobiography of Richard Baxter* abridged by J.M. Lloyd Thomas, Dent, 1974

Beck, William and Ball, Frederick: *London Friends' Meetings,* F. Bowker Kitto, 1869

Besse, Joseph: *A Collection of the Sufferings of the People Called Quakers*, Luke Hind, 1753

Bishop, George: *The Throne of Truth Exalted Over the Powers Of Darkness,* Giles Calvert, 1657

Bittle, William G: *James Nayler 1618-1660, The Quaker Indicted by Parliament*, Sessions, 1986

Blome, Richard: *The Fanatic History*, J. Sims, 1660,

Braithwaite, William C.: *The Beginnings of Quakerism*, Sessions, 1981

Brink, A.W., *Paradise Lost and James Nayler's Fall*, Journal of the Friends Historical Society 53.1 (1972), p. 106

Brockbank, Elisabeth: *Edward Burrough: A Wrestler for Truth*, Bannisdale, 1949

Burton, Thomas: *Diary*, Henry Colburn, 1828

Byrne, Richard: *Prisons and Punishments of London*, Harrap, 1989

Carlyle, Thomas (ed.): *Oliver Cromwell's Letters and Speeches*, Literary Licensing LLC, 2014

Clarendon, Edward: *Selections from Clarendon*, Oxford, 1955

Cooke, Robert: *The Palace of Westminster*, Macmillan, 1987

Crawford, Patricia: *Women and Religion in England, 1500-1720*, Routledge, 2014

Crouch, William: *Posthuma Christiana*, J. Sowle, 1712.

Damrosch, Leo: *The Sorrows of the Quaker Jesus*, Harvard, 1996

Dawson, William Harbutt: *Cromwell's Understudy: The Life and Times of General John Lambert and the Rise and Fall of the Protectorate*, William Hodge, 1938

Deacon, John: *The Exact History of the Life of James Nayler*, Edward Thomas, 1657

Dormandy, Thomas: *The White Death: A History of Tuberculosis*, Hambledon, 1999

Durston, Christopher: *Cromwell's Major-Generals*, Manchester University Press, 2001

Ellwood, Thomas: *The History of Thomas Ellwood*, J. Sowle, 1714

Evelyn, John: *The Diary of John Evelyn*, Everyman, 2006

Farmer, Ralph: *The Great Mysteries of Godliness and Ungodliness*, William Ballara, 1655

Farmer, Ralph: *Satan Enthroned in his Chair of*

Pestilence, Edward Thomas, 1657

Farr, David: *John Lambert, Parliamentary Soldier and Cromwellian Major-general, 1619-1684,* Boydell, 2003

Fox, George: *The Journal of George Fox*, Everyman, 1924

Fox, George: *A Warning to All in this Proud City called London*, 1654

Gardiner, S.R.: *Oliver Cromwell*, Kessinger, 2004

Gaunt, Peter: *The English Civil Wars 1642-1651*, Osprey, 2003

Gibb, M.A.: *John Lilburne the Leveller: A Christian Democrat*, Lindsay Drummond, 1947

Gregg, Pauline: *Free-Born John: A Biography of John Lilburne*, Everyman, 1986

Grigge, William: *The Quaker's Jesus*, M. Simmons, 1658

Higginson, Thomas: *A Brief Reply to some part of a very scurrilous and lying Pamphlet, called Saul's Errand to Damascus*, 'T.R. For H.R.', 1653

Hill, Christopher: *The World Turned Upside Down*, Penguin, 1984

Hobbes, Thomas: *Behemoth* (Clarendon Edition Of The Works Of Thomas Hobbes): Volume 10, Oxford, 2014

Hopper, Andrew: *'Black Tom': Sir Thomas Fairfax and the English Revolution*, Manchester University Press, 2007

Hutton, Ronald: *The Rise and Fall of Merry England*, Oxford, 1994

Ingle, H. Larry: *First among Friends: George Fox and the Creation of Quakerism*, Oxford, 1996

James, William: *The Varieties of Religious Experience*, Longmans, 1913

Johnson, Samuel: *Lives of the Poets: Milton*, Oxford, 1953

Knox, R.A.: *Enthusiasm*, Oxford, 1950

Latimer, John: *The Annals of Bristol in the Seventeenth Century*, William George's Sons, 1900

Lynch, John: *Bristol in the Civil War,* The History Press, 2009

Marriott, Brandon: *Transnational Networks and Cross-Religious Exchange in the Seventeenth-Century Mediterranean and Atlantic Worlds,* Routledge, 2016

Mcconville, Sean: *A History of English Prison Administration*, Routledge, 2015

Matthews, Ronald, *English Messiahs*, Methuen, 1936

Moran, James: *Printing Presses*, Faber, 1973

Neelon, David: *James Nayler in the English Civil Wars*, Quaker Studies, Volume 6, issue 1, 2002

Parker, Geoffrey: *Global Crisis: War, Climate Change and Catastrophe in the 17th Century,* Yale, 2014

Peters, Kate: *Print Culture and the Early Quakers*, Cambridge, 2005

Picard, Liza: *Restoration London,* Phoenix, 2003

Porter, Stephen: *Pepys's London*, Amberley,

2012

Punshon, John: A Portrait in Grey, QHS, 1984

The Rider of the White Horse, Thomas Underhill, 1643

Roberts, Keith: *Cromwell's War Machine: The New Model Army, 1645-1660*, Pen & Sword, 2005

Ross, Isabel: *Margaret Fell: Mother of Quakerism*, Longmans, 1949

Rowse, A.L.: The England of Elizabeth, Reprint Society, 1953

Sessions, William K: *Early Quaker Printing*, Sessions Book Trust, 2006

Smith, *Bernadette: Martha Simmon[d]s 1624-1665*, Sessions, 2009

Taylor, Ernest E: *The Valiant Sixty*, Bannisdale, 1951

Vane, Henry: *The Retired Man's Meditations, or, The Mystery and Power of Godliness*, EEBO, 2010

Vipont, Elfrida: *George Fox and the Valiant*

Sixty, Hamish Hamilton, 1975

Webb, Simon: *Deep Roots? A Fresh Look at the Origins of some Quaker Ideas*, Langley Press, 2013

Whittier, John Greenleaf: *Old Portraits and Modern Sketches*, Hardpress, 2016

Whitehead, George: *James Nayler, the Quaker Jesus: An Impartial Account of the Most Remarkable Transactions Relating to His Life*, Langley Press, 2016

Yelyr, R: *The Whip and the Rod*, Read Books, 2013

Selected Works by James Nayler, or Contributed to by Nayler

An Answer to a Book Called The Quaker's Catechism, London, 1656

A Short Answer to a Book called The Fanatic History, Giles Calvert, 1660

An Answer to the Book Called The Perfect Pharisee, 1654

A Collection of Sundry Books, Epistles, and

Papers, Repressed, 2015

A Discovery of the First Wisdom, Giles Calvert, 1653

O England, Thy Time is Come: London, 1656?

Glory to God Almighty, Thomas Simmonds, 1659

The Power and Glory of the Lord Shining out of the North, Giles Calvert, 1653

Saul's Errand to Damascus, Giles Calvert, 1653

To Thee Oliver Cromwell, Giles Calvert, 1655

Website

The Works of James Nayler (Quaker Heritage Press): www.qhpress.org/texts/nayler

For free downloads and more from the Langley Press, please visit our website at:

http://tinyurl.com/lpdirect

70464577R00158

Made in the USA
Columbia, SC
07 May 2017